Reviews for:

Absolute Security:
Theory and Principles of Socially Secure Communication

Absolute Security: Theory and Principles of Socially Secure Communication should be considered required reading for anyone focused on secure and private communication. In this book, Alan Radley makes sense of the complexities which ordinarily restrict this topic to IT people only. What's more, Alan's no-nonsense approach and fearless honesty, is refreshing. I recommend this to everyone who is interested in making certain that their communication is more private, secure and resilient.

Bill Montgomery - CEO Connect In Private Corp.

Excellent read! Succinct and accurate on a subject that normally wanders into tangential discussions confusing and diffusing the goal. Radley breaks down today's hottest topic in a way that provides reference to students as well as guidance to the more learned. Absolute Security will give you an optimistic understanding that, even in an ever-increasing world of digital surveillance and criminal threats, ... **absolute security** is eminently achievable... I found it spot on and a fine addition to the body of work on cyber-security but specifically to the discussion of privacy within communications... I see this short book as a reference document for students studying cyber security as well as an excellent read for CTOs, CSOs, CISOs, and CEOs laboring over how to analyze their needs for increased security. Absolute Security allows you to hit the highlights or dive deeper into the subject with your many charts, diagrams, and glossary of terms. Well done.

Vic Hyder - Chief Strategy Officer at Silent Circle.
Commander, U.S. Navy (SEAL), retired.

As cyber education evolves to meet the pace of change in our digital world so does the need for good reference books. Absolute Security is a timely and spot on publication that I shall be recommending to my students; well done Dr Radley.

Professor Richard Benham
Professor in Residence,
UK National Cyber Skills Centre.

If Only We Had Taller Been - by Ray Bradbury

The fence we walked between the years did bounce us serene.
It was a place half in the sky where,
   in the green of leaf and the promise of peach,
   we reached our hand and almost touched the sky.
If we could reach out and touch, we said,
   it would teach us not to, never to, be dead.
We ate, and almost touched that stuff;

Our reach was never quite enough.
If only we had tallied then, and touched God's cuff, his hem.
We would not have to go with them, with those who had gone before.
Who, short as us, stood tall as they could and hoped that by
   stretching tall that they could keep their land, their home,
   their hearth, their flesh and soul.

But they like us were standing in a hole.
Oh Thomas! Will a race one day stand really tall,
   across the void across the universe and all?
And measure all with rocket fire.
At last put Adam's finger forth as on the Sistine ceiling.
And God's hand come down the other way
   to measure man and find him good?

And gift him with forever's day.
I work for that, for that short man, large dream.
I send my rockets forth between my ears.
Hoping an inch of good is worth a pound of years.
Aching to hear a voice cry back across the universal mall.

   We've reached Alpha Centauri!
      We're tall!
         My God! We're tall!

The purpose of this book series is to explore how...

Computers can give *Humans* the Ability to:
Think / Act - *Freely, Ethically and Optimally*
(and for the true benefit of all)

Opened up are blueprints, visions and dreams of the relationship(s) between man and machine; and through the eyes of visionaries, writers, and thinkers from throughout time.

In 1970, Sir Lewis Mumford, said:

> The most disastrous result of automation, then, is that its final product is Automated—or Organisation of—Man... he who takes all his orders from the system... and who cannot conceive of any departure from the system... a whole race of acquiescent and obedient human automatons... and a cult of anti-life begins at this point.

According to Mumford, a mechanised dystopia can be avoided; but we must engage in *information pooling*—sharing all the ideas of humanity. Here the ideas, goals and habits of a society are aligned with industrial processes; and by machines that foster: collective freedom of thought/action.

The path to a better world begins by recognising and cataloging the ways in which we are today: not free. Unfortunately man's most precious gift, his *very thoughts*; are too-often censured, isolated and controlled (partly through computers); and increasingly in disturbing ways that tend to enslave him. Accordingly, we list examples of the ways in which automatic systems limit human potential; and explore how computers may—in the future—be used to set us free.

Discussed is an alternative approach to the computers of tomorrow, whereby the wishes, plans and actions of society may be aligned to benefit all. Clarified are the relationship(s) between the design of computers and—ultimately human made—social policies / decisions / outcomes. Cross your fingers.

Alan Radley - Blackpool, UK.

P.S. Along the way we see...

... a panoply of computer secrets / designs / inventions.

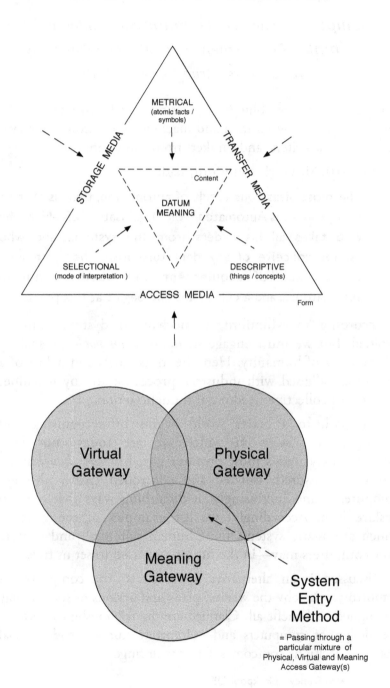

A B S O L U T E

S E C U R I T Y

THEORY

and

PRINCIPLES

of

SOCIALLY SECURE COMMUNICATION

A L A N   S T U A R T   R A D L E Y

for Mum and Dad

and dedicated to:

Kim, Francisco, Restie and Rowena,

Ruth, Chris, Nigel and

Philip, Ellen, Nigel, Arlene, Joshua,

Emma, Ben, and Caroline Radley.

If privacy is outlawed, only outlaws will have privacy.
— Philip Zimmermann

The chances are your data was leaked this year.

In 2014 alone, more than **one billion personal records** were
illegally accessed -- including health, financial, email and
home address data, and other personal information.
[Source: ZDNet.com (January3rd, 2016)]

www.alanradley.com | www.keymail.info

Absolute Security: Theory and Principles of
Socially Secure Communication
ISBN 978-1523408061 (Paper - Black and White)
First Edition [Version 35] Fonts: Adobe Garamond Pro, Gill Sans, Nunito, Helvetica.
49,684 words - 28 illustrations [UK spellings]

Contents

Preface

THE IDEA for the present series of book(s) grew out of a keynote presentation that I gave at the *Fourth International Workshop in Human-Computer Interaction, Tourism and Cultural Heritage* in Rome, Italy on September 25th 2013. My talk was entitled: *Computers as Self*; and concerned: moves away from the self and moves towards the self; and in relation to computer system design, use and application.

I had summarised the historical, present-day and potential future aspects of the interrelationship(s) between self and computer; but my paper only scratched the surface of a vast and important topic. The ways in which we design, develop and use computers, have far-reaching implications for the future of humanity—and related questions are of momentous import.

In fact, as we become ever more involved with, and dependent upon, computers; it may be that our essential nature is being shaped and/or changed as a result. It is prescient therefore to study the features of an emergent phenomenon; the *self as computer* (merging of self with computer), and in terms of a deeper, broader and more comprehensive inquiry.

Ergo we can learn:

who we were, who we are and who we may become.

Our thesis concerns the nature of mankind's relationship(s) to/with machines. Many writers have speculated on utopian and/or dystopian futures as a result of technological advancements.

It is useful to study the history of technological progress in this respect, and not only to discover why each scenario may come to pass, but also to learn how we can better chart the path ahead. Probable is that our survival and ultimate destiny as a species, depend on the development of appropriate technologies—and especially computers. Thus careful planning is essential when it comes to our technological future.[1]

We must 'study' the future intently, and consider the potential rewards and hazards of each scenario.[2] To get the ball rolling, we present an overview of blueprints, visions and dreams with respect to possible future computer-worlds. Accordingly, we formulate a strategy for an ideal human-computer relationship, and postulate a society so arranged as to benefit all; named the *technopia*.

A key feature of the technopia is the establishment of natural human rights—techno-rights—with respect to a technological society; combined with appropriate and human-centric information usage; and so to ensure that machines: interact harmoniously with humanity.

Norbert Wiener urged us to *ask the right questions* with respect to machines, and this book is an attempt to do the same. Our approach is to find human-centric solutions for the problems of an increasingly computer-centric future.

But the future is at the same time marvellous and dreadful, known and unknown.

---

[1] It is not in the stars to hold our destiny but in ourselves. – William Shakespeare

[2] Destiny is not a matter of chance; it is a matter of choice.
It is not a thing to be waited for, it is a thing to be achieved. – W. J. Bryan

The issues are complex because technological issues are intermingled with social, economic, and environmental ones etc. Yet the stakes are so high, that it is beholden on each writer to make his position known.

Paramount, in my view,

are three broad-ranging initiatives:

- Thought freedom / equality / ownership (individual & collective)
- Atomic organisation of, and free access to, all knowledge
- Open + private publication of thoughts / ideas / votes

Thought-ownership is key, in order to ensure that the thinker is rewarded for useful contributions, and not punished or disadvantaged in any way. Knowledge should be free and open, accessible and flowing everywhere and anywhere without limitation—whereby all open-thoughts are visible to everyone.[3]

Unfortunately, current systems fail to provide for the frictionless creation, publication and use of ideas. Thus careful planning is essential when it comes to our technological future. Questions are easy to spot for today's systems. For example; are the amalgamated ideas of humanity not the shared heritage of every new born child? Where is the world-library and/or universal knowledge repository? Who builds today's systems, and in what sense are they useful and/or democratic? Do we have equality of access to ideas—or honest self-expression?

If some humans are spied upon, but others are not, then by definition we do not have equality of expression.

---

[3] Sharing of private-thoughts / data - securely - is also a fundamental human right.

Are some humans more equal than others?

Do we have—in any sense—sufficient access to the deep and parallel structure(s) of all human knowledge? Is technology evolving by itself, and according to an anti-humanistic agenda? Do certain dark agendas shape computer system design/usage?

Overall, are we allowing: *the wishes of the few to outweigh the needs/wishes/rights of the many?*

Finding the answers is challenging. Certain experts proclaim the existence of technological barriers as justification for why humanistic systems cannot ever be built. Others cite economic and/or security barriers.

Problems do exist, but we must not use the same as an excuse to block the path to authentic and people-centric technologies. Despite optimism, we live in dark times. Increasingly there is a movement towards centralisation of computing resources. Authorities attempt to justify why we cannot ever be allowed to share ideas (plus votes) openly and/or privately.[4]

Are we to accept these self-appointed parties—with self-given powers—as *god-like beings*; who judge, rule and punish the *rest of us* on a whim?

Like Beyonce, we ask: who run(s) the world?

We might not the like the answer(s), or what they say about human freedom(s) in the year 2016. Conversely, we postulate a new type of atomic-network that provides for an open sharing of ideas.

---

[4] Man alone can enslave men. – Simone Weil

A *'World-Brain'* is the result; comprising massively distributed thought-atoms (hyper-thoughts) which offer boundless mechanisms for the creation, preservation, retrieval and sharing of content (ideas, opinions and votes).

George Orwell said: if you want a picture of the future, imagine a boot stamping on a human face—forever.

Orwell's nightmarish world is one of *newspeak, thought-crimes, memory-holes, double-think, and of clouded-perception*; whereby thoughts are constantly observed, twisted, negated and used to eliminate free-will/truth. Systems and machines are used to subjugate man. Foucault likewise imagined super-panopticon surveillance machines that may be used to curtail human freedoms. Hopefully we can avoid such big-brother scenarios, but we must not: throw the responsibility onto the machine.

Another prescient comment comes from Lord Bertrand Russell, who said: Machines are worshipped because they are beautiful, and valued because they confer power; they are hated because they are hideous, and loathed because they impose slavery.

The quote is apt. Computers are resplendent machines—with high levels of apparent intelligence; independent decision making ability (seemingly); and—most implausibly—motivations of their own; but they are also, ultimately, human creations. This is an obvious statement of fact, but less clear is why we should all (collectively) allow computer systems to be designed that, in actual fact; restrict freedoms, limit access to knowledge, and favour minority interests.

Observe that...

Artificial Intelligence is false;

and machines simply obey our commands.

My thesis shall be that design of computers is unquestionably; design of the whole arena of human life, and therefore, in a real sense, design of self. Needed is careful planning, to ensure that humans be the masters—not of each other—but of our machine slaves, and it must not turn out to be the other way around!

Today computers continue to develop in a technical sense, with ever faster processors, and new form-factors etc. However technological mastery remains illusory; related to the biggest problems. In this respect, I am not (unlike some) waiting for the emergence of an all-powerful God-computer that will save man from himself; but I do have faith in a bountiful—*but planned*—technological destiny for us all.

It is my hope, that you will find the discussion(s) enclosed herein - not only interesting - but thought-provoking.

Ideally, the book may prove to be of some practical usefulness. In this respect, I am crossing my fingers!

Thank you for your kind patience, I remain, yours truly,

Alan Radley

Dwell on the beauty of life...

Watch the stars, and see yourself running with them.

– Marcus Aurelius

It has become appallingly apparent that our
technology has exceeded our humanity.
- Albert Einstein

Acknowledgments

I ACKNOWLEDGE ALL of the friends, mentors, writers, teachers and others who took the time to time to impart various nuggets of wisdom. Full copyright is acknowledged (where known) for all works, and quoted in the list of captions or else the original publication is given or else the publication date is provided wherever possible.

Thanks to Professor Kim Veltman, Professor Francisco V. Cipolla-Ficarra, Dr Ted Nelson, Dave and Rose Gentle, Restie and Rowena Wight, Philip, Ellen, Nigel, Arlene, Joshua, Emma, Ben, and Caroline Radley, Nigel Pugh, Clark Hood, Ruth Grundy, Chris Green and others. Special thanks to Ruth Grundy, Chris Green, Nigel Pugh, Bill Montgomery, Frank Rowland, Vic Hyder, Ross Johnson, Richard Vizor, Michael Krausz, Julian Cordingley, Eugene Panferov, Christian Rogan, Vitali Kremez, Professor John Walker, Sean McGurk, Ahmed W, Troels Oerting, Kent Schramm, Peter E. Sand, Dr Merrick S. Watchorn, Richard Stiennon, Daniel McGarvey, Bruce Roberts, Ricardo Baretzky, Kevin T. McDonald, Jim O'Conner, Jonathan Trull, Marcus H. Sachs, Subrahmanya Gupra Boda, Ross Johnson, Sunil Varkey, David Jordan, Pantazis Kourtis, Benoit Piton, Graham Thompson, Martin Lee, Utkarsh Sinha, Dr Rizwan Ahmad, Laszlo Dellei, Ratan Jyoti, Tony Robinson, Ido Naor, Anthony Scarola, Stuart Naisbett, Anand R. Prasad, Kevin Hickey, Allan Watt, Jonathan Coombes, David Marugan, Dave Brown, Martin Visser, Michael Lester, Paul Kearney, Michael Hopkins, Cedric Thevenet, Colonel John Doody, Paul Crespo, Richard Redditt, Alex Smirnoff, Patric J.M. Versteeg, Christophe Duhamel, Arno Brok, Peter Bassill, Tony Collings (OBE) and Professor Richard Benham for reading / correcting / discussing the manuscript - and for supplying expert advice / support / inspiration.

Author's Credentials

Alan Radley is a writer, inventor and generalist / technologist who is based in the UK. Alan holds a Bachelor's degree in Astronomy, and also a Doctor of Philosophy (Ph.D.) degree in Physics (from University College London); plus he has two Master's degrees: one in Spacecraft Technology and another in Business Administration. He has worked as a research fellow at University College London and as a research scientist for the European Space Agency and NASA. Alan is a regular public and keynote speaker, and he has taught over 500 students on undergraduate and postgraduate courses in physics, astronomy, and computing.

Alan has written 10 books himself, and he has been co-editor and co-author of 5 Handbooks on Computing published by Blue Herons Press. Alan's book 'Self as Computer' has been nominated for the Ludwik Flek Prize for the 'best book in the area of science and technology studies' by the Society for the Social Studies of Science (4S). Alan is on the editorial advisory board for the AInCI Computing Handbooks; and is the author of 10 papers in this series; the latter being for the International Association of Interactive Communication (AInCI); where he has been on the scientific committees for 12 international conferences, workshops and symposia held / planned in Rome, Venice, Toronto, Madrid etc between 2013-2016.

Alan was granted a patent for his Hologram Mirror in 2009. He has developed three main software designs in C++ and Java; named Spectasia, GlobalOpt and KeyMail; and he wrote these programs himself—amounting to some 250,000 lines of code. In summary, Alan is an evangelist for the ethical, moral and spiritual dimensions of computers, systems and machines.

Chapter One

Introduction

THE SUBJECT AT hand is the secure transfer of meaning between individual human beings - using networked computers. Our goal is to characterise a point-to-point communication system for replicating *information patterns* - encapsulated as discrete units of data *(messages / files / folders)* - between remote computer nodes; whilst protecting the social integrity (privacy) of said patterns in place and time. A second goal of this book is to establish a safe procedure for point-to-point information transfer - and by means of logically consistent definitions, analysis and exposition.

Professor Donald MacKay (1922-1987) once said that the informational content of a message / representation consists of three components; **metrical, descriptive**, and **selectional**. Accordingly, in terms of the point-to-point transfer of information units (datums) between two humans - or the one-to-one replication of meaning from a sender to receiver - we can differentiate between the information pattern that is sent (i.e the atomic, symbolic and/or *metrical* data being replicated - the digital 0s and 1s etc), and the *descriptive* and *selectional* capacity of the receiving human.

N.B. In the present book we explore just one of 12 security sub-system types (communication of private-datums): wherein we discuss transfer of private datum-copies existing on a point-to-point communication system (whilst superficially considering aspects of data storage and presentation wherever necessary). Other sub-system security measures may be necessary in a real system - and in order to protect standard computer processing, storage and presentation operations; and not only for private datums but for secret and open datums as well (see Appendix L).

In other words, the receiver engages in a process of interpretation by utilising his or her '***beholder's share***'. Hence the meaning of a message is crucially dependent on the specific way(s) in which the receiver interprets the message. Ergo, effective and efficient communication between two parties depends (or relies) upon a certain degree of synchronisation and agreement in terms of factors such as *language, experience, truth, history,* plus *mode* and *context* of the communication process itself.

We begin with a simple question - ***what is security*** - in-and-of-itself - and especially in terms of digital information sharing? In order to be able to formulate an answer we must narrow our field of study - and concern ourselves solely with person-to-person (point-to-point) information transfer. We differentiate this topic from all other information transfer types which involve a source-point and end-point that is not (in and of itself) a human being. Ignored methods include *machine-to-machine, machine-to-person,* and *person-to-machine* techniques. In other words; we are not concerned with those cases where a computer initiates transfer(s) of information between machines, or does so automatically from machine to human or vice-versa.[5]

---

[5] N.B. Most principles - discussed herein - for private / secure point-to-point information transfer - apply also to these other communication types.

N.B. In the present book we place emphasis on human-to-human communication(s) - noting: 1) that whilst we recognise that interpersonal communications by means of networked computers obviously relies on a combination of several human-to-machine and machine-to-machine communications etc; it is our view that these other considerations relate largely to lower-level system-implementation details - and the fundamental 'aims' plus functionality of any system must always be dictated from above (or at the level of human concern(s)); and 2) that any full consideration would include all aspects of the 12 security sub-system types and would likely see the present book growing to over 1000 pages in length.

We exclude from our discussion all systems of public information sharing (i.e. *open-datums*) and social networks whereby the information transfer is one-to-many, many-to-one or many-to-many. Accordingly, **security** - for a person-to-person communication system - can be defined as **protection** of *secrecy*, *privacy* or *openness of meaning*; or the safe transfer of single / multiple datum(s) between humans.

In this context, **privacy** implies that:

• A communication system exists that connects humans together via **socially restricted access-nodes;**

• The source datum (+ meta-data) is sent from sender to receiver node as a single or **uniquely accessible** copy;[6]

• Both **access-nodes** may serve as **memory-nodes** for the datum, so long as socially unique access is preserved;

• The datum is protected from unwarranted social access **(i.e. who can see, know & change it)** by the system;

• Protection of datum access is for specified place(s) and time(s) and to achieve a state of persisted privacy.

< {1} We submit that the aforementioned predicates for secure and private communication - are true, valid, consistent, self-evident and complete. Q.E.D. >

---

[6] In this context - 'uniquely accessible' refers to protection of Social Accessibility Status (or Privacy Status (i.e secret, private, or open status)) for the communicated datum; whereby (within the boundaries of) the communication system - no change(s) to the pre-existing privacy status can happen (it is immutable).

It is salient (for upcoming discussion(s)) to consider how we obtain access to items in the real-world. To begin with, we: A) look for the item - or scan a scene - and in order to identify the desired thing and so to discover its whereabouts (whilst correctly distinguishing the item from background clutter). Next we: B) Move towards the item or a navigate a path to its location - before grasping / touching it (whilst avoiding any path-blocking objects / overcoming movement difficulties); and finally: C) we study/map/open-up the item - and in order to understand its contents and/or meaning (may require prior knowledge / special techniques and/or unlocking methods / key(s)).

Prior to the widespread adoption of the Internet - information assurance concerned reliable data storage/processing. But today, whilst data backups etc are still vital, security is more often associated with **data communications security.**

Meaning / Communication

A concept or **datum** of any idea or thing is a **pattern of meaning**, an abbreviated description, definition or set of 'facts' concerning the thing in question; typically prescribing an event, object, feeling, etc.; in token of, as a sign, symbol, or evidence of something.

A **communication system** is a system or facility for transferring datum(s) / patterns-of-meaning between persons and equipment. The system usually consists of a collection of individual communication networks, transmission systems, relay stations, tributary stations and terminal equipment capable of interconnection and interoperation so as to form an integrated whole.

Social Access

The ability of a person to **see, know** and/or **change** a datum's form and/or content.

Privacy [cp. Secrecy = datum is accessible by only one person]

A **private-thought/datum** is distributed / available to a limited number of people; and hence some form of **social sharing (& trust)**, plus **protection** is implied; and in order to prevent it from morphing into an open-thought/datum.

Protect = Lock, Block or Conceal an item.

Lock - unsafe-actor(s) cannot **open/know** an item's form/content.

Block - unsafe-actor(s) cannot **reach/grasp** an item's form/content.

Conceal - unsafe-actor(s) cannot **see/find** an item's form/content.

Security = Protect access to an item. **Access** = find, contact and/or know an item. **Possess** = **find** (see/locate) plus **contact** (reach/grasp/hold) an item.

In this book we shall define certain terms, concepts and principles related to digital information sharing; as (partially) taken from the book *'Self as Computer'* and the keynote paper: *'Humans versus Computers, Systems and Machines; A Battle for Freedom, Equality and Democracy'*. In those publications a distinction has been made between three kinds of human thoughts: **secret**, **private** and **open**.[7]

Accordingly, we now define a process of secure information transfer - that consists of private data shared during a one-to-one information replication.

We begin by identifying a **secret-datum** (analogous to a *secret-thought*) - which has not yet left the source-point (or sender's mind); and which is assumed to be unique in that nobody else can know (or discover) the precise **form** or **content** of the datum at the source-point. Once the datum arrives at the destination-point; it is a **private-datum**; because it now exists - ostensibly solely - as an identical copy in both locations simultaneously (it is a *private-thought*).

As an aside, an **open-datum** is one that anyone may access - but *open-thoughts / datums* are not a subject of this book (see the companion book *'Self as Computer'*).

---

[7] In the present context - a **secret-datum / thought** has restricted access - and is limited to a single person; whereas a **private-datum** is accessible only to a specific group of people (N.B. access = who can see, know and/or change the item).

Lock = Ofttimes there is a difference between **having** and **knowing** an item. Locking creates a gap / barrier or unbridgeable chasm - between possession and full understanding - for unauthorised parties - and especially for meaning of information.

Henceforth adjudging that a point-to-point communication is private and secure; is equivalent to saying that the original unit of meaning existing at the 'source' node has, as a result of the one-to-one replication, only one accessible copy - at the 'receiver' node. Furthermore this copy is - unequivocally - accessible only by the (trusted) human for whom the communication was intended (i.e. it is access-controlled).

We call such a process *single-copy-send* - or *socially secure communication* - whereby the process of communication may itself be private (no public meta-data exists); and there is no possibility of any nth-party obtaining a copy of the communicated datum. A party might be able to guess the contents of the datum - or presuppose that the sender / receiver parties possess it and/or have exchanged it - but that is altogether different from certain knowledge.

It seems prudent - at this point - to ask another straight-forward question; specifically:

What is the nature - and architecture - of secure and private cyber-communication?

In actual fact - answering this key question - will be the primary task of this short book; but we can begin our exploration of related topic(s) thusly...

Information Security, sometimes shortened to **InfoSec**, is the practice of defending information from unauthorised access, use, disclosure, disruption, modification, perusal, inspection, recording or destruction. It is a general term that can be used regardless of the form the data may take (e.g. electronic, physical).

For a Secret-Datum, socially secure communication restricts access to just one person. Hence the sender and receiver are the same person; and the system simply 'memorises' the datum.

INTRODUCTION 7

Firstly, we define:

- **Human Communication** = Transfer of discrete package(s) of meaning - messages - between people; or the one-to-one replication of datum(s) between minds + nominal meta-data (perhaps).

- **Socially Secure Communication** = Communication that protects socially restricted access (secrecy or privacy) for the replicated meaning - datum(s) + nominal meta-data (perhaps).

- **Open Communication** = Communication that protects socially open access for the replicated meaning - datum(s) - and also any meta-data for the communication process itself (perhaps).

- **Single-Copy-Send** = Communication of a datum (+ meta-data) with guaranteed social security.

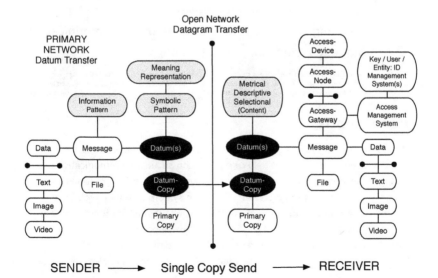

See: John R. Coyne: 'Self-Aware Software
Components-Records Management' and
related publications (Patent: US8144941 B2).

The only truly secure system is one that is
powered off, cast in a block of concrete
and sealed in a lead-lined room with
armed guards. – Gene Spafford

Primary Copy

N.B. We recommend reading Appendix L AND M
(PAGES136-143) before starting Chapter 2: regarding
absolute security: definition(s) + target / method(s).

A **primary-copy** is a place-holder for a private datum of
meaning - existing within the boundaries of a point-to-point
communication system; whose content and form are
restricted in terms of **social access** (i.e who can see, know
& change the same); whereby the datum is (ideally)
communicated via **single-copy-send** from the source-point
to any (and all) designated receiver-point(s).

Secondary Copy

N.B. Legitimate secondary copies are compatible with
single-copy-send because - for example - a central-server
network creates (ostensibly private) secondary copies to
facilitate off-line data sharing / storage.

A **secondary-copy** is a replication of a primary-copy - existing
within (or outside) the boundaries of a point-to-point
communication system - that may be **legitimately** produced
by the communication process itself; and/or be **illegitimately**
created as a result of the unwarranted activities of a hacker.

Tertiary Copy

N.B. Tertiary copies (whilst nefarious) are compatible with
socially secure communication or single-copy-send - because for
example - the datum-copies may be protected from
unsafe-actors by means of strong encryption and/or coding etc.

A **tertiary-copy** is a replication of a primary or secondary
copy - which is generated post-communication by
extracting datum(s) from a large body of communication
data (e.g. a transatlantic data pipe).

N.B. Christian Rogan pointed out to me that the peer-to-peer primary communication copy is also
(from one perspective) the true version/copy, which leads to another solution often described as
Self-Aware, whereby the object (file or data) enforces its own security protocols/policies (see top-left).

Formalism

Our goal is to bring **formalism** to a field that doesn't even have one - that is to
bring unity and order - to the field of information-security (communicative-aspects).
Strangely absent - is any kind of top-level theory, and missing are fundamental
definitions and/or first-principles etc. Ergo, the system-designer's job becomes one
of - collecting **partial formalism(s)** - before somehow stitching them together.
The net result is - partial truth(s) and/or sub-optimal approaches - or at least major
difficulties. Conversely, we seek to establish a **foundational framework** for the entire
field of: information-security; and by means of comprehensive / holistic perspective(s).

Chapter Two

Why

Security

is

All About Copies

I N THIS SECOND chapter we overview methods for achieving privacy in terms of our interpersonal communication(s). Building on the security definitions established in the first chapter; we hereby characterise privacy as being concerned primarily with exposed copies of the communicated datum (+ meta-data). Therefore cybersecurity vulnerabilities may be mitigated by social restriction - and protection - of such copies.[8]

A second goal of this chapter is to list and classify, plus compare and contrast, the different kinds of threats and attack-vectors / surfaces that may exist for a digital point-to-point communication system.

---

[8] How many copies are there? Where are the copies? Who can see, know and/or change a copy, and how long do copies hang around?

Accurate determination of social accessibility protection - or Security Status (for a datum-copy) - or judging whether an (ostensibly) private-datum has been communicated with absolute or partial / absent security - may sometimes be difficult to achieve with any degree of confidence / assurance.

If you think technology can solve your security problems, then you don't understand the problems and you don't understand the technology. – Bruce Schneier

Form and Content

Privacy Status (for a datum-copy) = legitimate social accessibility status (i.e secret, private, or open) [see top-right page 18].
Security Status (for a datum-copy) = protected / unprotected > privacy status.

A **datum** is a discrete pattern of meaning that may be transferred between minds (network access-nodes). A **datum-copy** is a particular instantiation of a datum's pattern - that exists inside or (potentially) outside of a point-to-point communication system.

A copy has two primary aspects: firstly **form** (the encapsulating format) - or **media** of storage, communication / delivery, and access; and secondly **content** (a representation with metrical, descriptive and selectional aspects). Creation of a datum-copy involves instantiation of form in place and time (i.e. illustration of content in the real and/or virtual worlds).

A datum-copy has a natural owner - often the sender / creator of the datum. Ownership rights include protection of social access (e.g. secrecy, privacy, openness) for the copy - in terms of who can **see**, **know** and/or **change** the content and/or form of the copy.

When we speak of - a datum-copy being **hacked** - that is defined as unwarranted social access to the informational content of the datum (i.e. loss of privacy). It may be that loss of privacy - extends also to aspects of the copy's form, but for the datum itself loss of privacy relates to - and consists of - purely informational content.

Digital Media

Digital-media are electronic media used to store, transmit, and receive digitised information; and may refer to any media that has been encoded in a machine-readable format. Digital-media - referred to here simply as **media** - can be created, viewed, distributed, modified and preserved on computers. For our purposes we have compartmentalised media into 3 types: **storage**, **transfer** and **access** - see related discussion on page 30.

In simple terms we can characterise private communication as being concerned primarily with protection of ownership right(s) for *datum-copies* - or management of safe: storage, transfer and access for replicated datum(s) (+ meta-data). Once we recognise that any potential copy has to be either - a *primary*, *secondary* or *tertiary* one - then we can develop a formula for what we might term absolute security.

Absolute security - for a point-to-point communication instance - is the replication of a single instance (or *primary-copy*) of a private-datum from one socially restricted access-node to another [ref. Absolute Security: TARGET][9]. In other words, it is the *single-copy-send* of a datum from one party to another; whereby no - socially accessible - nth-party copies exist whatsoever (hopefully persistently).

Likewise we can define *partial / absent security* as the existence of any unprotected - or nth-party accessible - *primary / secondary / tertiary datum-copies*. Both of these metrics - [absolute] and [partial / absent] security - are mutually-exclusive true / false values for any act of communication. It is obvious that just because a *datum-copy* has (apparently) been communicated with absolute security at one epoch; then that does not mean that such a status will necessarily be permanent.

---

9 See Appendix M: Definition of Absolute in the Context of Security.

The OED (2nd Edition) - lists for Copy: 1) A transcript or reproduction of an original. 2) A writing transcribed from, and reproducing the contents of, another; a transcript. 3) Something made or formed, or regarded as made or formed, in imitation of something else; a reproduction, image, or imitation. (e.g. electronic, physical).

Long-term systematic vulnerabilities and/or unknowable threats may emerge at other place(s) / time(s) - and expose previously hidden / protected copies to unwarranted social access. All kinds of hardware / software, networking and social influencing factors can affect the privacy status of a primary, secondary and/or tertiary copy. Potential vulnerabilities include exposed: *user IDs, logins, passwords, and private encryption keys, meta-data etc;* and each may contribute to privacy breaches.

We are now in a position to classify the different ways in which a hacker could potentially gain unwarranted access to a primary, secondary or tertiary copy of a ***private-datum***. Obviously, in order to improve the security of any communication system; one seeks to reduce the number of - ***attack-surfaces*** - and related ***attack-vectors*** (for datum-copies) - and so to minimise the opportunities for break-ins to an (ostensibly) secure network.

Accordingly, we now define the principal ways in which a nominal - or generalised - communication system may be compromised; and hence result in a data-breach. At least eight kinds of hacking / spying / eaves-dropping methods are possible; as listed on the right.

In the computer security context, a **hacker** is someone who seeks and exploits weaknesses in a computer system or computer network. Hackers may be motivated by a multitude of reasons, such as profit, protest, challenge, enjoyment, or to evaluate those weaknesses to assist in removing them.

Typical 'hacking' methods...

- ### Cloud provider legal request - 'back-door'
  - primary / secondary copy

- ### Transmission provider legal request
  - primary / secondary copy

- ### Transmission line reconstruction (remote)
  - tertiary copies

- ### Communications hacking (local and remote)
  - primary / secondary copy

- ### Communications eavesdropping (environment)
  - primary / secondary copy

- ### Cloud account hacking - 'front-door'
  - primary / secondary copy

- ### Physical device hacking
  - primary / secondary copy

- ### Physical device data replication
  - primary / secondary copy

Access (General) = Find, Contact and/or Know an Item.

Find - actor can **see/locate** an item's form/content (cf conceal).

Contact - actor can **reach/grasp** an item's form/content (cf block).

Know - actor can **understand/open** an item's form/content (cf lock).

Obviously, depending upon the nature of a particular breaching technique, different impacts arise - on the primary, secondary and/or tertiary copies - as to whether or not a system is vulnerable at any particular place / time. Dependent variables include: *degree of access of the attacker to local resources, relationships of attacker to/with 'nth' parties, motivations / capabilities of attacker, attack / defence techniques, system and network vulnerabilities, and the capabilities / legal operating frameworks - plus assumptions - of all the parties involved.*

Note that for the purposes of our analysis, we make no distinctions (legal or otherwise) between an ordinary attacker; and one who may possess any supposed: *legal, moral, and/or ethical right(s)*; in relation to gaining unauthorised access to a *private-datum* (see ethical discussion in chapter 10).

Finally, and given what's been said; I do find myself wondering how - or even if - it is possible to mount an effective defence - permanently - against any and all cyber-attacks.[10]

---

[10] In the OED (2nd Edition); **private** and/or **privacy** is defined thusly:

1) In general, the opposite of public. 2) To keep private; to seclude. 3) The state or condition of being withdrawn from the society of others, or from public interest; seclusion. 4) The state or condition of being alone, undisturbed, or free from public attention, as a matter of choice or right; freedom from interference or intrusion. Also: 5) Private or retired places; private apartments; places of retreat.

The Absolute Security: TARGET - for a point-to-point communication system - is the replication of a single instance (or *primary-copy*) of a datum - from one socially restricted access-node to another. In other words, it is the *single-copy-send* of a datum from one party to another; whereby no - socially accessible - nth-party copies exist whatsoever (hopefully persistently).

Chapter Three

Aetiology

of a

Secure Network

THE SUBJECT AT hand is network design for secure transfer of meaning between individual human beings. Our goal is to characterise a computer network for replicating datum(s) - safely - between remote computer nodes; whilst protecting the social integrity (privacy) of said datum(s) in place and time.

A second goal of this chapter is to introduce the two basic kinds of computer network; and to identify key principles of secure network design; and by means of logically consistent performance metrics.[11]

---

[11] Remember that earlier, we had defined **security** as **protection of privacy, openness or secrecy of meaning** - for a datum-copy. The Oxford English Dictionary - or OED (2nd Edition) - offers up the following entries for **security**: 1) the condition of being secure; 2) The condition of being protected from or not exposed to danger; safety. And also: 3) Freedom from doubt; confidence, assurance. Now chiefly, well-founded confidence, certainty.

A datum-copy's Security Status - or protected social accessibility status - specifically its absolute or partial / absent security value - may be either: A) determined / known; or else: B) undetermined / unknown at a particular epoch.

Passwords are like underwear: you don't let people see it, you should change it very often, and you shouldn't share it with strangers. – Chris Pirillo

Computer Network

A **computer network** is a telecommunications network which allows computers to exchange data. In computer networks, networked computing devices exchange data with each other along network links. The connections between nodes are established using either cable or wireless media.

Datum Immutability

A **datum's** content may have a purely informational meaning **(be descriptive)** and/or a purely logical meaning **(be functional)** - or posses a combination of both kinds of meaning - according to context of use. However, the process of point-to-point transfer of a datum; is (normally) defined to be a transfer of information alone - and the datum is **immutable**.

Copy Mutability

Replication of a **primary-copy** (datum from + content) is transfer to a destination-point. It may be that a copies form **(encapsulating media of storage, communication / delivery, and access etc)** changes during replication - hence copies are **mutable**.

Lock, Block or Conceal [i.e. Prevent: knowing, contacting or finding]

There are basically 3 ways to defend / protect an item in the real-world.

For example, when protecting an entrance to a house (i.e. walled safe) - we can:

A) **Lock the entrance** and **armour reinforce it** - or make it difficult to open/know;

B) **Block the entrance pathway** - by preventing an attacker from reaching it - for example by placing objects in the entrance-way - or by **eliminating** it altogether;

C) **Conceal the entrance** - and make it difficult to see / find.

Similarly for datum-copies / attack-surfaces - we can protect these in analogous way(s).

Backdoor - refers to either: 1) A tool installed after a compromise to give an attacker party easier access to the compromised system around any security mechanisms; or 2) A secret entry method into a system (developed by a system manufacturer/owner) which gives access by nth-parties (typically the police) to private-datums (unbeknown to the owner of said private-datums).

We begin by considering security for a primary-copy; whereby a private-datum is made available on a local **access-node** within the primary-network - and by means of an **access-device** (i.e. a personal computer) connected to the Internet (i.e. an **open-network**).

Previously, for an act of private communication, we had assumed that a local access-node provided socially restricted access to primary-copies.

However such a statement is predicated on the fact that each access-device affords an **actor-coherent** defence against any data-breaches - successfully. Unfortunately this may be a rather big (i.e. false) assumption; because access-device security depends upon a mishmash collection of protective methods provided by network administrators, operating system and device manufacturers etc.

Use of the term 'network' - is problematic to say the least. This is because an access-device may be open to the data-processing activities of (any number of) inter-relating **local-actors** plus **network-actors** (i.e. human / automated ones etc). Ergo **hybrid-actors** are formed that may be partially / fully invisible, overly complex, and/or unknowable in some way - and which may be - as yet - only potentially present.

A **computer virus** is a program that, when executed, replicates by inserting copies of itself (possibly modified) into other computer programs, data files, or the boot sector of the hard drive. Viruses often perform some type of harmful activity on infected hosts, such as stealing hard disc space or CPU time, accessing private information, corrupting data, displaying political or humorous messages on the user's screen, spamming their contacts etc. N.B. A virus conceals the fact of its execution from a user. This is what distinguishes a virus from a trojan - a user is unaware of running a virus.

A datum-copy's Privacy Status (i.e secret / private / open accessibility status); works together with its Security Status (access protection) to perpetuate and defend the datum's inner meaning.

Hardware is easy to protect: lock it in a room, chain it to a desk, or buy a spare. Information poses more of a problem. It can exist in more than one place; be transported halfway across the planet in seconds; and be stolen without your knowledge. — Bruce Schneier

Network Types

The datum-copy's Privacy Status - may be either: A) legitimate (i.e posses secret / private / open status); or B) illegitimate (i.e fall into an undefined / hybrid category whereby privacy status is unknown / compromised / changeable / unpredictable).

From the perspective of a digital communication system - named a **primary-network** - we can identify two basic network sub-types. Firstly we have **cloud-server networks**; such as email, Dropbox, Facebook, Twitter etc; in which all of the communicated data is relayed by - and stored on - centralised storage facilities.

Secondly we have **Peer-to-Peer (P2P) networks**; such as Napster, BitCoin, BitTorrent etc; the same forming a distributed network of peer-to-peer nodes that render the communicated information directly available to network participants - without the need for centralised co-ordination.

A key advantage of P2P is that:

Participating users establish a virtual network, entirely independent from the physical network, without having to obey any administrative authorities or restrictions.

Whilst it is not my intention to unduly simplify the inherent (and mammoth) complexity of computer networking as a topic, or else to disregard the great diversity of hybrid network types that are possible; space limitations preclude any further analysis of network design in terms of implementation details.

One-Time-Pad

In this encryption technique, a plaintext is paired with a random secret key (also referred to as a one-time pad). Then, each bit or character of the plaintext is encrypted by combining it with the corresponding bit or character from the pad using modular addition. If the key is truly random, is at least as long as the plaintext, is never reused in whole or in part, and is kept completely secret, then the resulting cipher-text will be impossible to decrypt or break. However, practical problems have (often) prevented one-time pads from being widely used.

Biometrics - Biometrics use physical characteristics
of the users to determine access.

We can identify two - enforced - coherency predicates for absolute security; namely: *actor-unity* (of purpose); and *actor-integrity* (of action); for safe hardware / software operations on each access-device. Similarly, *unsafe-actor* repellent / containment techniques can be used to preserve the legitimacy of data-processing operation(s) on the primary-network.

Moving on to consider security for the primary-network - plus any *secondary-network(s)* - or privileged-access networks intimately connected to the same - we are concerned here with secondary-copy protection. Accordingly, for those situations that require absolute security; it would seem to be good practice (at least in general) to reduce the number of legitimate secondary-copies - and thus to minimise the number of exposed attack-surfaces. Attaining adequate protection for any illegitimate secondary-copies and/or tertiary-copies; requires specialist data-encryption, plus identity and access management techniques.

And that's about it for now.

We have identified key principles of safe network design. Remaining is to 'explode' said factors; and to bring *visibility*, *clarity* and *predictability* to all of the relevant *actors*, *entities* and *processes*, plus *attack* and *defensive methods*, present.

Of course, all this good practice goes right out the window as soon as a trusted insider (like Snowden) goes rogue or is compromised. Two or even three factor authentication - something you **know** (password), something you **have** (MAC address, private Key) and/or something you **are** (finger-prints, retina scan etc) - can also greatly slow-down or prevent unauthorised access.

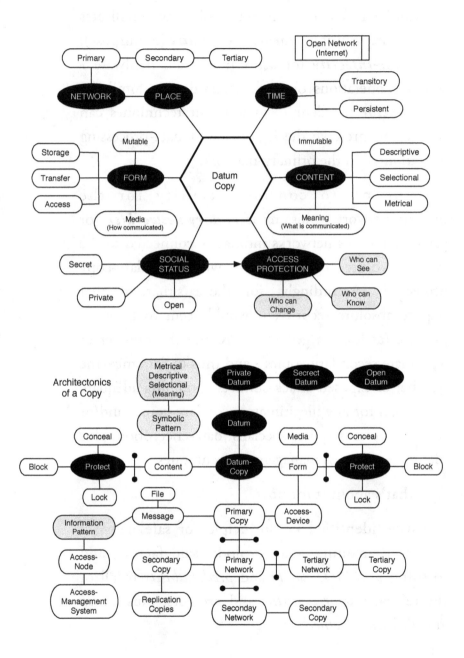

Figures 2 & 3: Datum-Copy on a Secure Point-To-Point Communication System

Chapter Four

Building

Actor-Coherent

Defences

T HE SUBJECT AT hand is the building of *actor-coherent* defences - with respect to the safe transfer of meaning between individual human beings.[12] Accordingly, we specify a nominal primary-network's data-processing stack; and with a view to obtaining absolute security for communicated datum(s). Security is **protection of privacy (of meaning) for a communicated datum**. Ergo, a second goal of this chapter is to identify - attack-surface type(s) - for said private-datum; and by means of logically consistent definitions, analysis and exposition.

---

[12] The OED (2nd Edition) lists the following for the entry '**meaning**':

1) That which is intended to be - or actually is - expressed or indicated. Alternatively: 2) Of language, a sentence, word, etc.: The signification, sense, import; a sense, interpretation. Also, 3) the intent, spirit as apart from the 'letter' (of a statement, law, etc.). 4) †(that) is to meaning: (that) means.

The mantra of any good security engineer is: **'Security is a not a product, but a process.'** It's more than designing strong cryptography into a system; it's designing the entire system such that all security measures, including cryptography, work together. — Bruce Schneier

Access Protection = Provision of: A) Defence-mechanism(s) to prevent unauthorised access; and B) Entry method(s) to facilitate valid entry.

Local Actor

A **local-actor** is a data processing unit - existing on a local access-device - comprised of either hardware and/or software / human elements — which (potentially) acts on a datum-copy's form and/or content within the primary-network's data-processing stack.

Network Actor

A **network-actor** is a data processing unit - existing on a remote networked-device - comprised of either hardware and/or software / human elements - which (potentially) acts on a datum-copy's form and/or content within the primary-network's data-processing stack.

Actor Coherence

An **actor-coherent defence** is when all of the actors, entities and processes - present in a primary-network's data-processing stack - are **impelled** to act together in order to protect the private datum-copy's form and/or content from unwarranted social access (hopefully for all places / times). N.B. An actor may originate - from either automated processes and/or human ones.

Defensive Mechanism(s)

A datum-copy - encapsulated on a media device - has 3 components: 2 related to **form**: the **physical-representation,** and the **virtual-representation,** and 1 related to **content:** which is the **meaning-representation** (with **metrical, descriptive** and **selectional** aspects). Ergo, there are 5 possible attack-surface types for each of 3 possible media of **storage, transfer** and **access** - leading to a grand total of 15 attack-surface types. However each surface may be protected by 6 kinds of protection (entry-method(s) + defence-method(s)): or **locking, blocking** and **concealment** mechanism(s); hence we can have up to 90 fundamental types of protection for a single copy (or a private datum).

The term *data-processing stack* refers to the sum total of all the actors, entities and processes etc; existing on - and/or potentially influencing - a primary-network's communication 'pipeline'. As previously indicated, this stack may involve hybrid-actors emanating from outside the primary-network - on secondary / tertiary / open-network(s) - including known and unknown, and desirable and undesirable, ones etc.

How can we get a grip on something so ephemeral?

We begin by identifying (potential) vulnerabilities on a supposedly secure communication 'pipeline'.

Attack-surfaces come in six basic kinds.

Firstly we have three related to the datum-copies *form*; or its encapsulating *media of storage*, *transfer* and *access*.[13]

Secondly we have three attack-surface types related to the datum-copies *content;* and these are the *metrical, descriptive and selectional* ones.[14]

---

[13] The author has compartmentalised media into 3 kinds; but as explained later - often real-world media are a combination of two or more types - for example central-server networks - which combine access, transfer and storage functions.

[14] See: **Information, Mechanism and Meaning** (MIT Press - 1969) by Donald M. MacKay. Whereby attack-surface types (our concepts) have been equated to Donald's: three kinds of information layer(s) present in any representation.

Unsafe-Actor: An actor (i.e. a program / human / process) existing on and/or influencing the data-processing stack that may be structurally - visible / invisible and/or known / unknown in terms of existence - but is **questionable / harmful** in terms of purpose, value, action and/or integrity - and hence may (potentially) cause undetermined / detrimental / harmful effects and/or progress unknown or undesirable programming path(s); or else provide unauthorised access to private-datum(s) etc. Whereby the term unsafe-actor encapsulates the meaning(s) of the term **threat-actor** and similar terminology.

Phishing is an example of particularly interesting hacking technique; whereby when the user clicks on a file thinking it will perform one specific action (e.g. opening a file) - it secretly or overtly does something entirely different!

Companies spend millions of dollars on firewalls, encryption and secure access devices, and it's money wasted, because none of these measures address the weakest link in the security chain. – Kevin Mitnick

Patently, the generalised locking, blocking and concealment tools/strategies apply not only to items - but also to processes and methods. But remember that these ideas are analysis tools - which may be mixed, interlaced, overlaid etc and so are not sharply defined physical laws!

Primary Network

The **primary-network** is a provided point-to-point communication system; whereby a private **access-node** (the source-point) exists on a networked **access-device**; which stores a primary-copy of a private-datum; prior to the single-copy-send of the same to a socially restricted access-node (the destination-point). A primary-network may create legitimate secondary-copies of the primary-copy.

Secondary Network

A **secondary-network** is a privileged-access network intimately connected to the primary-network's communication pipeline; whereby copies of communicated private-datum(s) may exist on an nth-party organisational network and/or various local and/or central replication (backup) network(s). A secondary-network may contain legitimate replicated secondary-copies of primary-copies and/or other secondary-copies.

Tertiary Network

A **tertiary-network** is not directly connected to the primary-network - but nevertheless may still (belatedly) access data traffic flowing across primary and/or secondary-networks - resulting in illegitimate **tertiary-copies** of primary/secondary-copies.

Access-Node / Access-Device

An **access-node** is a virtual access gateway (i.e. legitimate login-node / point-of-entry) for a primary/secondary/tertiary network; and is normally used (only) by an authorised party to gain entry to said network. An **access-device** is a physical access device that enables a human to gain entry to the same network (i.e. a personal computer).

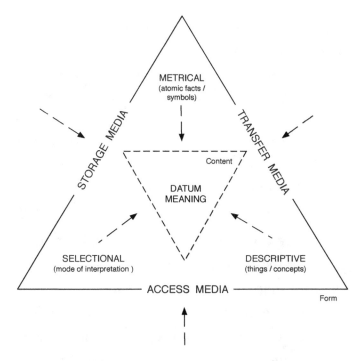

Figure 4: Attack-Surface Types (Datum-Copy)

An ***actor-coherent*** defence guarantees that all actors present on a primary-network's data-processing stack work-together to protect the privacy of a datum's content. Two kinds of operational strategies exist for achieving an actor-coherent defence. Firstly, we can attempt to identify ***unsafe-actors*** and limit their harmful activities - but this may be extremely difficult to do - since actor types are numerous and many are unknown / remote / hidden.

Polymorphic Code / Attack(s)

A **polymorphic code** is code that uses a polymorphic engine to mutate while keeping the original algorithm intact. That is, the code changes itself each time it runs, but the function of the code (its semantics) will not change at all. For example, 1+3 and 6-2 both achieve the same result while using different code. This technique is sometimes used by computer viruses, shell-codes and computer worms to hide their presence.

Secondly, we can move all copies (or attack-surfaces) beyond the reach of any harmful actors - still a difficult process - but at least the copy types are known - and hence (potentially) defendable. Normally we employ both techniques (to the same effect); but in our thesis we shall emphasise the latter approach - protecting copies from attack. Illustrated below is a generalised hacking procedure - but bear-in-mind that all defensive strategies relate to protection of either *form* or **content** (for a datum-copy).

Any attack begins with form. Logically, an intruder must possess a means of engaging with (one or more) of the encapsulating: *media of storage, transfer and/or access -* for a primary, secondary or tertiary copy. Accordingly, the attacker (and his 'helper' actors) must first connect with the private copy's *physical-representation* - and by opening-up an electronic / magnetic / optical 'container' - in order to obtain a *virtual-representation* of the copy.

Next because the copy has been transposed into a storage / transmission / presentation format; the virtual representation must be processed to extract the inner datum(s) - or *meaning-representation* (normally). Ergo protection of a form based attack-surface - implies preventing / blocking any unsafe-actor(s) from gaining unwarranted access to (opening-up) the physical and/or virtual representation(s) of the copy (see later chapters).

Concealment: We have the **target** (item to be concealed); and the concealment **method**. Whereby there are two basic kinds of concealment structural targets: **existence** of the item, and **content** or inner meaning. Structure can be concealed in 3 ways: A) conceal form itself; or B) conceal location (where); or C) conceal location (when): item time-span, duration or persistence. Whereby there are 3 basic processes (for each method): A) *conceal by transformation* of form/location; or B) *conceal by similarity (equivalency)* - that is by hiding an item alongside a large number (of ostensibly identical) items; and C) *conceal by difference (complexity)* - or hiding an item amongst a large number of greatly/potentially varying forms/structures.

The next task is to extract meaning from datum content. Remember that a representation has metrical, descriptive and selectional aspects. Notably, the metrical aspect - or pattern of atomic facts / symbols - is always present - and works together with a descriptive aspect - to convey meaning. The so-called *metrical attack-surface* may be protected (for example) by means of encryption *(entry locks + content concealment)* - or obfuscation of symbolic structure - and so that only an actor with the correct key(s) can decode the underlying symbolic pattern.

Once the metrical layer is decoded, we must match each symbol to its specific meaning - and according to the common descriptive language employed - named the *descriptive attack-surface*. Notably the sender and receiver may be using an obscure coding language whereby the symbol-to-meaning relationship is protected (i.e. RED means BIG etc). Finally, modal context(s) - named *selectional attack-surface(s)* - may protect constructive aspect(s) of the representation.

Do not worry if this chapter seems overly theoretical - all will become clear soon enough - because we are now in possession of all the principles needed to specify absolute security [ref. Absolute Security: TARGET and METHOD(S)].[15]

---

[15] In this book, we focus on identification of first-principles for privacy / security - as opposed to mathematical explanations and/or low-level system design constructs. See Appendix L and M: Definition of Absolute Security.

In communication, a **code-word / code-group** is an element of a standardised code or protocol. Each code-word/group is assembled in accordance with the specific rules of the code and assigned a unique meaning. Code-words are typically used for reasons of reliability, clarity, brevity, or secrecy.

Securing a computer system has traditionally been a battle of wits: the penetrator tries to find the holes, and the designer tries to close them. — Gosser

The whole notion of passwords is based on an oxymoron. The idea is to have a random string that is easy to remember. Unfortunately, if it's easy to remember, it's something nonrandom like 'Susan.' And if it's random, like 'r7U2*Qnp,' then it's not easy to remember. — Bruce Schneier

How long before we see all kinds of underground and illicit new Internet communication systems - like TOR - which use their own packet routing protocols and unbreakable defense systems - and to escape oversight?

Attack Surface

An **attack-surface** is an exposed facet / system entry-point for a datum-copy, existing on a primary-network's data-processing stack, and which (potentially) facilitates unwarranted social access to a private datum-copy's content and/or form.

Attack Vector

An **attack-vector** is a specific data-processing path, existing on a primary-network's data-processing stack - which (potentially) provides unwarranted social access to a private datum-copy's content and/or form.

Access Gateway

An **access-gateway** consists of one or more access-nodes and/ or exposed attack-surface(s) - for a primary, secondary or tertiary copy. The gateway is comprised of a group of hardware / software elements that together form an 'entrance aperture' for actor pathway(s). The gateway may be - open or shut - visible or invisible - protected or unprotected - at any particular place / time - and for specific actor(s) / attack-vector(s) - and by means of access / locking mechanism(s).

Representation Aspects

We have characterised a datum-copy - as a representation consisting of 3 aspects: firstly the **physical-representation** (or encapsulating media of storage, transfer and access for the datum-copy); and secondly the **virtual-representation** (datum-copy in a storage, transfer, and/or access format); and finally the **meaning-representation** (a datum with metrical, descriptive and selectional layers). N.B. All three layers are not-necessarily present/protected for a particular copy. For example, you can have a physical-representation - but no format (meaningless data). Or else a copy with encrypted metrical structure (i.e. locked + concealed); but no unusual descriptive structure(s), that also uses standard modeless structure(s) - hence no descriptive / selective protection.

Chapter Five

Primary-Network

Design

T HE SUBJECT AT hand is the design of a *primary-network* - with respect to the safe transfer of meaning between individual human beings. Accordingly, we specify the component(s) of a nominal primary network's data-processing stack; and with a view to obtaining absolute security for communicated datum(s) [ref. Absolute Security:TARGET].

A second goal of this chapter is to identify safe principles of design / operation - for a primary-network - and by means of logically consistent definitions, analysis and exposition.[16]

---

[16] A quick reminder of purpose is useful; because in this book, we are simply attempting to define: **Absolute Security (see Appendix M)**. A quick glance at the word **'define'**; in the OED (2nd Edition); provides the following listings: 1) To bring to an end. To bring to an end (a controversy, etc.); 2) to determine, decide, settle. 3) To determine the boundary or spatial extent of; to settle the limits of. Also fig. 4) To determine, lay down definitely; to fix, decide; to decide upon, fix upon. 5) To state precisely or determinately; to specify.

Security by Obscurity: 'Incidentally, it did occur to me that the whole CVE disclosure process shows how reliant we currently are on security by obscurity (that is so frowned on by experts). Our unintentional and unavoidable reliance on it will continue to be our main and implicit defence until we find a way to write software that is inherently automatically secure.' - Personal communication from Nigel Pugh (February 17th 2016) [see page 30 for CVE]

Malicious Code: Software (e.g., Trojan horse) that appears to perform a useful or desirable function, but actually gains unauthorised access to system resources or tricks a user into executing other malicious logic.

Data exfiltration is the unauthorised transfer of sensitive information from a target's network to a location which a threat actor controls. Because data routinely moves in and out of networked enterprises, data exfiltration can closely resemble normal network traffic, making detection of exfiltration attempts challenging for IT security groups.

Media Types

A **storage-media** is a bundle of hardware / software technologies that work together to form a memory system - and in order to persist a datum-copy's form and content. Example types include: hard disc drives, solid state drives, optical drives, magnetic drives, and cloud storage systems like Dropbox, iCloud, and Google-Drive etc.

A **transfer-media** is a bundle of hardware / software technologies that work together to form a delivery system - and in order to send a datum-copy from a source-point to a destination-point. Example types include any data transfer system consisting of telecommunication components such as wired and/or wireless links, data channels etc; including low level protocols such as LAN, WAN, FTP, HTTP and high level protocols like email etc. The definition would include networked applications like DropBox, Google-Drive etc.

An **access-media** is a hardware / software system that enables an actor to see, know and/or change a copy's form and/or content (e.g. a data-access terminal).

N.B. Real-world media are normally an amalgamation of all three media types - **storage, transfer** and **access**. However blending media types / functions unnecessarily can be a source of security problems. For example, any superfluous mixing of the transfer and storage functions - may lead to exposed datum-copies at undesirable place(s) / time(s). In our terms, it is a question of how best to preserve socially secure communication.

CVE Identifiers: The Common Vulnerabilities and Exposures (CVE) system provides a reference-method for publicly known information-security vulnerabilities and exposures. MITRE Corporation's documentation defines CVE Identifiers as unique, common identifiers for publicly known information-security vulnerabilities in publicly released software packages. The National Cybersecurity FFRDC, owned by The MITRE Corporation, maintains the system, with funding from the National Cyber Security Division of the United States Department of Homeland Security. CVE is used by the Security Content Automation Protocol, and CVE IDs are listed on MITRE's system as well as the US National Vulnerability Database.

In previous chapters we emphasised the need to bring actor-coherence to a primary-network's defences; and in terms of protecting the *data-processing stack* from the unwarranted activities of any unsafe-actors (i.e. automated and/or human ones). Accordingly, it is useful to identify the specific features of a nominal attack-surface, which (in any way) relate to exposure of a private-datum's form and/or content.

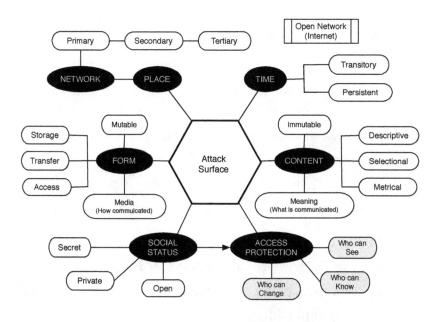

Figure 5: Attack Surface as Datum-Copy

There are basically two kinds of concealment targets; you can either focus on concealing structure - or else encourage the observer to look elsewhere (still a form of concealment). Whereby either the onlooker: A) Does not know **where** or **when** to look for an item (target location obfuscation); or secondly: B) finds that looking does not reveal **how** to find the item (target form confusion); or finally: C) Is encouraged to look **elsewhere** than an item's true location (observer misdirection - i.e. concentrate on directing the attention of the observer - using decoys and/or false targets - or hide messages in innocuous content etc). [see also concealment discussion on pages 26, and 76-77]

Masquerade Attack: A type of attack in which one system entity illegitimately poses as (assumes the identity of) another entity.

A physical-gateway defines a set of possible entry-method(s) for 'grasping' a digital-copy; and examples include valid and invalid access-nodes (logins), illicit software CVE break-ins, (successful entry-method(s): viruses, trojans, hacking etc), plus stolen CDs, hard-drives, and computers etc; including any and all ways of obtaining access to the container - or outer form - of the copy.

We can begin by characterising an attack-surface as equivalent to an exposed datum-copy (see figure 5).

For absolute security, we must protect:

[A] **Physical-Gateway(s)** - who can obtain a physical copy

[B] **Virtual-Gateway(s) -** who can open a virtual copy

[C] **Meaning-Gateway(s)** - who can decode datum(s)

To be successful, an intruder must first pass through the physical and virtual gateway(s); prior to deciphering the meaning of the inner datum(s) - or passing through any meaning-gateway(s) that happen to be present. Obviously a variety of different kinds of primary-network designs are possible - each with a specific feature set; but which one is safest? In order to find out - we can take a step-by-step approach to protecting access-gateway(s) for a nominal network.

In terms of securing *physical-gateway(s)* - or *locking / blocking / concealing* - all access-gateways/pathways related to the copy's physical representation - we can (perhaps) begin by eliminating all legitimate secondary-copies.

Copies and Attack-Surfaces

In this book, we have characterised all attack-surfaces as being (in one way or another) equivalent to an exposed datum-copy. In one respect - this is correct - and because any (successfully exploited) attack-surface must provide a pathway to a copy - and thus can be equated to an exposed facet of the copy - as it comes to exist on the communication system. However in another sense - it is obvious that not all attack-surfaces are copies - for example system-logins (access-nodes), access-devices, plus exposed communication data - are all (potentially) illicit windows into the system that may allow an unsafe-actor to access a primary, secondary or tertiary copy.

This can be done by moving to a **Peer-to-Peer** (P2P) network (no central copies) - assuming that no other organisational / transfer / replicated copies exist on any secondary-network(s) (see later chapters). Next we can focus on removing any possibility of an unwarranted nth-party producing illegitimate secondary / tertiary-copies. Here we rely on securing the datum's content during live transport. Special line-encryption / packet-scrambling methods can be used *(transport locks)*; in addition to moving the communication channel out-of-reach of an attacker - by means of closed physical and/or concealed ***virtual gateway(s)*** *(blocking / existence concealment)*. For example, we can use invisible / transitory access-node(s); secret protocol(s), private servers / packet-routing mechanism(s), and/or covert access-device(s) with hidden / spoofed **IP / MAC** data.

Remaining is a single class of attack-surface - primary-copies. In some ways this type of attack-surface is the most difficult to protect; because an access-device/node is analogous to an armour reinforced bank vault. Whereby once an attacker is inside the vault - he/she (normally) has free access to all of the valuable items. Unfortunately there are many ways for an attacker to break into this type of 'vault' - or access-node/device. Normally we must rely on a mishmash collection of (protected) physical / virtual gateways provided by network administrators, system manufactures etc.

Copy at-rest / in-transit: A datum-copy which is at-rest has a physical form that (normally) exists as an integrated unit of static information - because it has been memory 'saved' on an electronic storage media. Conversely, a datum-copy that is in-transit is moving (and possibly segmented) across a telecommunications line etc.

However due to the evolving nature of the risk; including newly discovered exploit(s), uncertain attack-vector(s) and countless hostile actor(s) etc; it is difficult to secure each access-node with full confidence over an extended period of time. One way to mitigate against such risk(s) is to move the access-node (plus associated private-copies/data-set(s)) - beyond the reach of an attacker. Ergo, we protect entry-method(s) - with valid access control(s) plus advanced encryption (i.e. locking all *virtual / meaning-gateways*).

Another way is to move the same to a secure portable device - with hidden IP / MAC addresses (i.e. closing / blocking / concealing *physical gateways*). In summary, access-gateways (for datum-copies) can be classified into three kinds: *physical-gateways, virtual-gateways* and *meaning-gateways*. Ergo gateway defences are predicated upon one - or more - of the following factors:

- Unbreakable (or strong) encryption/coding for copies;

- Secure Entity / Access / ID: Management System(s);

- 'Stealth' network design features.

All three predicates assume a primary-network with unimpeachable operations that provides socially secure communication for shared datum(s).

Ergo, we know *what* is required for absolute security - next we must prescribe *how.*

Chapter Six

Encryption

Theory

T HE SUBJECT AT hand is protection of *metrical attack-surface(s)*; with respect to the safe transfer of meaning between individual human beings. Accordingly, we specify how to protect symbolic structure (for datum(s)); and with a view to obtaining unbreakable encryption for datum-copies.

A second goal of this chapter is to define and classify encryption mechanism(s) for primary-network defence (i.e. locking datum-copies) - by means of logically consistent definitions, analysis and exposition.[17]

---

[17] N.B. Whilst in this book we have apparently overlooked **Identity and Access Management Systems** - plus **Secret-Key Management / Identity Authentication / Validation Techniques** - this is not so - and because most of the security and privacy techniques listed here which relate to the safe: transfer / storage / access of datum(s) - apply also to User-IDs, passwords, entity-identification, logins and Keys etc. Additionally, the problem of identity / key assurance is cyclic/nested in nature - whereby one has to either trust the (nth-party) party supplying / approving the item - or else defer to yet another (trusted) authority. Ultimately, it is the user himself who approves a party - or source / destination point - and/or a copy / key / certificate - by implicitly / explicitly trusting - a particular validation method.

ETEE example = Encrypt data at source with personal / user-owned key.

End-to-End Encryption (ETEE) is a system of communication where only the people communicating can read the messages. No eavesdropper can access the cryptographic keys needed to decrypt the conversation, including telecom providers, Internet providers and the company that runs the messaging service.

Semiotic Theory

In semiotics a **sign** is something that can be interpreted as having a meaning, which is something other than itself, and which is therefore able to communicate information to the one interpreting or decoding the sign.

Charles Peirce (1839-1914) developed a triadic theory of semiotics in which a sign is - a relation between the **sign vehicle** (the physical form of the sign), a **sign object** (the aspect of the world that the sign carries meaning about), and an **interpretant** (the meaning of the sign as understood by the interpreter).

Icons, Indices, Symbols

Signs are either icons, indices or symbols. **Icons** signify by means of similarity between sign vehicle and sign object (e.g. a map), **indices** signify by means of a direct relation of contiguity or causality between sign vehicle and sign object (e.g. a symptom), and **symbols** signify through a law or social convention (i.e letters / words present in a language).

Lock / Block / Conceal - Access Protection Mechanism(s)

It is possible that you may experience confusion - in relation to the application of the 3 protective methods - lock, block, conceal - to the safeguarding of a datum-copy. Just for clarification - herein whenever we speak of a **locking mechanism** for a datum-copy (existing on a specific media of storage, transfer and access) - what we are saying is that the **lock** prevents the **knowing/opening action** (i.e for datum access) - by some **protected entry-method** plus **defence-method(s)** (i.e. password entry-system (lock) plus **content concealment** of symbolic structure). Alternatively, **existence concealment** prevents an unsafe-actor from **seeing/finding a copy** by means of an **entry-method** that is itself secret/hidden (i.e. unusual descriptive coding) and/or secret/hidden **defence-method(s)** (e.g. possibly identical to entry-method). Likewise for blocking actions etc. Obviously there is overlap (and nesting) between the concepts of lock, block and conceal - but it is often useful to open-up protection - as a concept - into such facets.

The topic at hand is creation of an impenetrable *meaning-gateway* - or protecting a datum-copy's metrical attack-surface (or symbolic structure) - whereby the same copy is either - A) *at-rest*; or B) *in-transit*. Wherein we assume that any physical and/or virtual getaways (or protective measures for the copies form) may be ineffective and/or could fail.

Right away - for a point-to-point communication system connected to an open-network - we acknowledge that a problem exists in terms of message / identity / key: authentication and signification; or making certain that the *Identity and Access Management System* assigns the same to the correct party. Placing these matters aside, we find that there are two basic kinds of symbolic encryption:

• **Symmetric-Key-Encryption**: the encryption and decryption keys are the same. Communicating parties must have the same key before they can achieve secure communication.

• **Public-Key-Encryption**: the (public) encryption key is published for anyone to use and encrypt messages. However, only the receiving party has access to the (private) decryption key that allows messages to be read.

Entry-Method / Defence-Method (ref Datum-Copy)

An entry-method is a system access pathway - or series of actions that must be performed by a human and/or helper actor(s) - to access a datum-copy (i.e. a primary, secondary, tertiary-copy). Whereby an **entry-method** (may) involve traversing several system gateway(s) - before opening up the datum's inner meaning. A defence-method is a system access pathway that is inaccessible to unsafe-actor(s). Wherein both the **entry-method** and **defence-method(s)** may be protected by **locking, blocking** and/or **concealment** techniques. N.B. An entry-method plus defence-method - may sometimes be the exact same sub-subsystem (i.e fulfil a dual purpose for any particular access pathway).

Nothing stops you placing lots
of chains around your safe.

Cypher-Alphabet - An alphabet
composed of substitutes for the normal
alphabet or the particular alphabet in
which the cipher is written.

Cryptography

Cryptography is defined as a secret manner of writing, either by
arbitrary characters in other than the ordinary sense, or by methods
intelligible only to those possessing a (private) key.

Symbolic Encryption is the process of encrypting symbolic messages
- or obfuscating datums consisting of patterns of symbols.[18]
Whereby information is encoded in such a way that only authorised
parties can read it - typically by replacing / jumbling symbols
according to a mathematical procedure which obscures the original
symbolic pattern. In an encryption scheme, the intended
communication of information, referred to as plaintext (i.e "Alan is
tall"), is encrypted using a special algorithm, generating cipher-text
that can only be read if decrypted (i.e. "Bmbo jl umm").

For technical reasons, an encryption scheme (for a metrical attack-surface)
normally uses a pseudo-random encryption key generated by an
algorithm. It is in principle possible to decrypt the message without
possessing the key, but, for a well-designed encryption scheme, large
computational resources and skill are required. An authorised party can
easily decrypt the symbolic message with the key provided by the
originator to recipients, but not to unauthorised parties.

---

[18] Wherein we use the term '**symbolic encryption**' in a subtly different manner
than in the normal sense; whereby we make a distinction between **cryptography**
and **coding**. Ergo, we define a **cypher** as a - secret way of writing by means of
unusual structures-of-symbols (symbolic obfuscation) - or the straightforward
'jumbling/transposition' and/or 'replacement/substitution' of letters and words in
(for example) - a text message - and according to an 'encryption' algorithm.
Whereas we define **coding** - as a disguised way of writing - by means of the
assignment of unusual coded meanings for words / concepts / sentences - or
employing standard/unusual symbols which map to non-standard ideas /
structures / datum meaning(s) (i.e non-symbolic obfuscation). N.B. Any
communication instance has twin aspects: 1) Message conveyance (transfer of
symbolic structure or metrical content); and 2) Mapping to underlying facts /
datum-meaning(s) - or descriptive content. Of-course the two aspects can overlap
and inter-penetrate - but it is often useful to separate the two.

CODE - (French, Latin: 'tree-trunk', 'writing tablet') - A method of concealment that
may use words, numbers or syllables to replace original words / phrases of a message.
Codes substitute whole words whereas ciphers transpose or substitute letters or
digi-graphs. Also a disguised way of evoking meaning (non-symbolic obfuscation).

Either symmetric / non-symmetric encryption may be used to develop effective cryptographic software - and standards are widely available for employing such techniques. However successfully using encryption to ensure security may be a challenging problem - and because even a single error in system design or execution can allow successful attacks. Sometimes an adversary can obtain unencrypted information without directly undoing the encryption (see the Trojan Horse / Traffic Analysis hacking method(s) as explained elsewhere).

Overall, we advise caution in terms of reliance on cryptography alone for protecting a datum's privacy.

In this chapter we are concerned with protection of **symbolic** structure - or meaning - for communicated datum(s); whereby the message is comprised of a specific pattern of symbols. Wherein we ignore the possibility of using **icons** and **indices** as signifiers - and because these topics are unusual and/or lie outside of our analysis (e.g. steganography). Obviously the remaining topic of **symbolic cryptography** is complex; and any adequate treatment would run to a book-length treatise.

How then, you may ask, is it possible in only a few pages to say anything consequential on such a highly technical subject matter?

The OED (2nd Edition) - lists for **Confidential**: 1) Of the nature of confidence; spoken or written in confidence; characterised by the communication of secrets or private matters. 2) **Confidential communication**: a communication made between parties who stand in a confidential relation to each other, and therefore privileged in law. Confidential relation: the relation existing between a lawyer and his client, between guardian and ward.

Quite simply, we can identify best practice in terms of logical premises / reasoning / appropriate-conclusions for achieving absolute security; and hence outline effective methods to protect the metrical structure of communicated datum(s). Ergo, we abide by the following cryptographic principles:

Principle A: **Virtual Message Tamper-proofing**: The **digital signature verification** and **encryption** must be applied to the cipher-text - **when it is created** - typically on the same primary-network used to compose the message - to avoid tampering (adequate locking - guarantees message integrity).

Principle B: **Physical Message Tamper-proofing**: Encrypting at the time of creation is only secure if the encryption device itself has not been tampered with (i.e. closed / blocked physical gateway(s) or device-integrity).

Principle C: **Employ Secret Keys**: Obey Dr Claude Shannon's maxim (i.e. Kerckhoff's principle); and assume that: '**the enemy knows the system**'. Avoid relying on **security through obscurity** and/or **security through minority** - in terms of assuming that the secrecy / uncommonness of system design provides unimpeachable protection (adequate concealment + locking).

Principle D: **Pattern Obfuscation**: Special encryption / coding / scrambling methods must be employed to prevent spies from deducing information from patterns present in the copy.

Confidential Information Security or **Transmissions Security** - is an approach to information security that attempts to avoid detection - in terms of usage / application - and by means of special stealth and/or primary-network design features that camouflage any and all communications data from any unauthorised observers. An electronic form of communication security similar to steganography. Transmission security tries to hide the existence of secret messages in electrical exchanges, whether or not they are encrypted. Towards this end - the communication system and related method(s), plus primary-network, communication(s) data, and meta-data etc; are all rendered invisible/undetectable.

Principle E: **Access-node / Key / ID Security:** Adequate access control methods must be employed to protect unwarranted access to any and all access-nodes, access-devices, keys, user IDs etc (adequate blocking + key concealment).

Principle F: **Viruses, Trojan-Horses:** Methods to eradicate Viruses and to prohibit Trojans misrepresenting as safe-actors - hence preventing unsafe-actors from gaining unwarranted access to copies / actors on the data-processing stack (adequate blocking).

Principle G: **Environmental Spying:** Methods to prevent spying on the primary-network through leaking emanations, including radio or electrical signals and vibration(s) etc.

The history of cryptography provides evidence that it is difficult to keep details of a widely used algorithm secret. Accordingly, only secrecy of the key provides security - and because a key is often easier to protect (it's typically a small piece of information) than an encryption algorithm, and easier to change if compromised. (N.B. See later chapters for the *defence-in-depth* - or *castle* - approach to comprehensive information security.)

And that's about it for now; in later chapters we go onto explore all of the issues raised here; and in terms of attaining *holistic*, *effective* and *broadly considered* cybersecurity policies.

Comprehensive Information Security - or Complete Information Security - is an approach to information security that takes a broad-ranging view of, and rigorous approach to, the subject; and places the CIA triad of **confidentiality, integrity** and **availability** at the heart of information security policy. These 3 factors are referred to interchangeably in the literature as security attributes, properties, security goals, fundamental aspects, information criteria, critical information characteristics and basic building blocks etc.

Brute Force: A cryptanalysis technique or other kind of attack method involving an exhaustive procedure that tries all possibilities, one-by-one.

Jargon-Codes - Open methods of linguistic concealment. A type of open code, the jargon code is not hidden by symbols or transposed letters. Rather, an innocent word or words replaces another term in a sentence constructed in an innocuous fashion.

Beholder's Share

Art historian Sir Earnest Gombrich (1909-2001) first defined the '**beholder's share**' - which states that our perceptual experience – depends on the active interpretation of sensory input. Perception becomes a generative act, one in which biological and sociocultural influences conspire to shape the brain's 'best guess' of the causes (and meaning) of its sensory signals - or in our terms the meaning of the symbolic message being communicated.

Language

A **language** is a systematic way to express thoughts, feelings and ideas; often defined as the whole body of words and methods of words used by a nation, people, race or 'tongue'.

Codes

In our lives we constantly send messages that consist of different signs. These messages are based on **codes -** culturally defined systems of relationships / rules that connect ideas together in pre-defined / socially agreed ways. Barthes claimed that there is "**no message without a code**".

Forward-Secrecy / Perfect-Secrecy

In cryptography, **forward secrecy** is a property of secure communication protocols; a secure communication protocol is said to have **forward secrecy** if compromise of long-term keys does not compromise past session keys. This means that the compromise of one message cannot compromise others as well, and there is no one secret value whose acquisition would compromise multiple messages. **Forward secrecy** can be achieved by A) using new keys for each communication instance; or B) using multi-layered encryption - and hiding long-term keys inside a layer protected by short-terms keys (other methods are possible). **Perfect secrecy** is when an encrypted message (or cypher-text) reveals absolutely nothing about the unencrypted message (or plaintext). **Perfect secrecy** is obviously a very difficult (if not impossible) feature to achieve in a practical system (see one-time-pads).

Chapter Seven

The Beholder's Share

(Unbreakable Codes)

THE SUBJECT AT hand is protection of descriptive and selectional attack-surface(s) - with respect to the safe transfer of meaning between individual human beings. Accordingly, we specify how to protect descriptive structure (for datum(s)); and with a view to obtaining absolute security for communicated datum-copy(s). A second goal of this chapter is to define and classify coding mechanism(s) for primary-network defence - by means of logically consistent definitions, analysis and exposition.[19]

---

[19] Philosophically speaking, when we turn our attention to the **Beholder's Share** - or the interpretive contribution of the observer (aka sender / receiver) - two vital aspects come to mind: 1) firstly, we have to admit that interpretation is always present (to a smaller or greater degree), and because it is the observer herself who determines / assigns meaning (ultimately) to a representation; and also 2): we cannot have protection of privacy without: A) in some way causing (aspects of) the interpretation (ref encryption/coding) to remain a secret known only to sender / receiver; and also B) we must align the interpretative contribution(s) of both sender / receiver perfectly.

Open-Codes - A code concealed in an apparently innocent message. Open codes are a branch of linguistically masked communications which includes null cyphers, geometric methods and jargon codes.

Dictionary Attack: An attack that tries all of the phrases or words in a dictionary, trying to crack a password or key. A dictionary attack uses a predefined list of words compared to a brute force attack that tries all possible combinations. **Hybrid Attack:** A Hybrid Attack builds on the dictionary attack method by adding numerals and symbols to dictionary words.

Descriptive / Selective Coding

Descriptive coding refers to the process of assigning a pattern of symbols to the specific meaning of the conveyed message (communicated datum(s)). For a message with no descriptive attack-surface; typically a common (or well-known) descriptive language is employed - and in order to achieve effective (open) communication. However when the sender / receiver wish to communicate privately (i.e. using single-copy-send); then unusual symbol-meaning relationships (codes) and/ or mappings can be employed. Typically use of a secret look-up table / coding-method is desirable - for example sending numbers instead of words - whereby the numbers (uniquely) match to a specific page off-set, line-offset, and word-position in (for example) the Bible. Wherein coding numbers begin / continue / end on pre-identified page(s) known only to the sender / receiver.

Selective coding refers to the process of protecting constructive aspects of the symbolic and/or descriptive components of the message by means of private modal context(s). There are a near infinite range of coding techniques for so doing; whereby the sender and receiver use an agreed coding mode according to some pre-agreed indices.

An example of combined descriptive plus selective coding - is sending the message "Alan is tall": in the form of the number sets: (1, 67, 14, 3); (6, 13, 2,7); (56,3,107,23); wherein each set refers to: secret look-up-table, page, line, and word-number.

YOU CAN BAKE A CAKE WITHOUT SUGAR AND NOBODY WILL NOTICE, UNTIL THEY ACTUALLY TRY IT. BY THEN IT'S TOO LATE.

Another variation of "The cake is a lie," - Wendy Nather, Research Director, Enterprise Security Practice at 451 Research, notes that the best cakes/companies have sugar/security baked in. "The typical reaction to missing security is to try to slap it on afterwards in the form of 'icing' (e.g., 'Can't we just put a firewall in front of it?')," noted Nather who believes that there are many security products that follow the "icing" model, such as web application firewalls. "It just isn't the same as baking the security in to begin with," said Nather. It doesn't take a malicious hacker to break "top of the cake" security, said Nather who noted, "My kids are very good at separating the icing from the cake."

The topic at hand is creation of impenetrable *descriptive* and *selectional gateway(s)* - or protecting a datum-copy's descriptive and selectional attack-surface(s) (i.e. defining language(s) used and/or coding structure(s) employed). Whereby the same copy is either - A) *at-rest;* or B) *in-transit.* Wherein we assume that any physical, virtual, plus (symbolic) meaning gateway(s) - may be ineffective and/or could fail.

Once again we are faced with a host of potentially useful techniques in terms of descriptive and selective coding. The large number of such combinations makes for a particularly useful set of protective measures - each with a high level of robustness and immunity to attack.

Whereby **the large number and great diversity of potential coding method(s)** helps to effectively cloak / obscure - said attack surface(s); and because an attacker has difficulty guessing which specific protective technique(s) may have been used - leading to significant obstacle(s) for breaking into the coded datum(s). However there is an important caveat here, in terms of any unbridled optimism with respect to coding methods. That is the susceptibility of all coding / encryption methods to attacks whereby a spy attempts to **deduce information** from patterns present in the copy.

Protection by Diversity is a fundamental principle for attaining secrecy/privacy; whereby we first block/bar entry to a private item by some defensive means or protective barrier. Next we build a window/door into the barrier that may be opened (i.e. know/open action) - but only by means of a fully/partially secret entry-method. The entry-method typically includes a mathematical / text value and/or locking key (i.e. a secret password) with a specific form known / available only to authorised parties - and that is difficult to attain/guess; whereby it is diversity (potential to have many different values) that protects the key from discovery/use by an attacker.

We can think of coding as a statistical technique. Ergo for any fairly long message of - for example - english text; if a consistent encryption and/or coding method is employed; then due to the (relatively) small range of letters / words / phrases present in the english language - it may be possible to use numerical / computationally intensive methods to discover, guess and/or decode the original message. We can conclude that no coding / encryption method is (by itself) absolutely secure against all possible attack-vectors.[20] Ergo, form based protection is desirable. Previously, we had identified core principles of system design for symbolic cryptography. Here in this chapter we wish to do the same for *coding methods* - defined as the generation of descriptive and/or selectional layers for a representation.

Note that we can also use special coding techniques and/or modal methods for protecting symbolic structure - but we normally assign the same to encryption as a topic in-and-of-itself. Right away we shall state that all of the vulnerabilities and principles for effective cryptography apply also to coding methods. The only difference is that coding methods may be superior for eliminating and/or reducing the possibility of an attacker deducing information from well-known and/or repeated patterns (i.e. phrases) present in the communicated datum.

---

[20] An exception to this rule might be the use of One-Time-Pads.

Codebook - Either a collection of code terms or a book used to encode and decode messages (non-symbolic obfuscation).
Code-names - Name concealments for a person or object / item etc.

Pattern obfuscation is a central concern in terms of achieving ***socially secure communication***. Basically we are in the domain of statistics - because no matter how clever / intricate and/or obscure the coding or encryption technique - it can often be broken - given sufficient time, effort and resources. Note however, that to break into a protected datum using statistical methods requires that a sufficiently large - homogenous coded-segment - or section of cypher-text / coded-text sample is available for analysis.

Ergo we wish to avoid: using identical natural-language constructs too-often in a long message; and/or use of the same coding method(s) continually. Plus we wish to avoid sending coded messages with common patterns that may be used to reverse-engineer the coded datum(s). In fact, this is how the German Enigma code was broken; whereby every message contained known words - 'Heil Hitler' - day after day.[21]

How can we mitigate such formidable risks? Quite simply, by using sufficiently obscure and intricate descriptive coding schemes and/or strong encryption methods; plus by using selectional content that varies sufficiently in terms of modal obfuscation.

---

[21] The Enigma machines were a series of electro-mechanical rotor cipher machines developed in the early to mid-twentieth century to protect German commercial, diplomatic and military communications.

Code-text - The result of encoding a given communication (the plaintext). Similar to cipher-text, code-text differs mainly in that a code, rather than a cipher, conceals the text. **Code-numbers** - Function like codewords when they replace the words of a plaintext message. **Code-words** - see page 27.

Ergo - for socially secure communication - we abide by - as many as possible of - the following coding principles:

[A] Employ effective **symbolic encryption**; including multi-layer encryption with new keys generated for each communication instance (i.e. use perfect-forward-secrecy).

[B] Employ obscure **descriptive coding** methods (i.e. one-time-pad(s) or perfect-secrecy).

[C] Employ variable **selectional coding** methods (i.e. multiple code-books in a single message); with constantly changing constructive pattern(s) for each message. (i.e. one-time-pad(s) or perfect-secrecy).

[D] Employ **safe pattern constructs**. Avoid sending identical (coded) natural-language constructs repetitively; pad the pattern(s) with NULLS or hide them; use varying constructive code(s).

[E] Rely on the **Beholder's Share** - employ covert and obscure methods for interpretation of meaning.

And that's about it for now; in the next chapter we explain - form based - defensive gateways.

Glibc: Mega-bug That Threatens Thousands of Devices: A major CVE computer security vulnerability has been discovered - with experts cautiously warning it could potentially affect hundreds of thousands of devices, apps and services. However, due to the nature of the bug, it is extremely difficult to know how serious the problem is. "Many people are running around right now trying to work out if this is truly catastrophic or whether we have dodged a bullet," said Prof Alan Woodward, a security expect from the University of Surrey. Google engineers, working with security engineers at Red Hat, have released a patch to fix the problem. It is now up to manufacturers, and the community behind the Linux operating system, to issue the patch to affected software and devices as soon as possible. In a blog post explaining the discovery, Google's team detailed how a flaw in some commonly-used code could be exploited in a way that allows remote access to a devices - be it a computer, internet router, or other connected piece of equipment. The code can also be within many of the so-called "building blocks" of the web - programming languages such as PHP and Python are affected, as well as systems used when logging in to sites or accessing email. - BBC News (17th February 2016)

Chapter Eight

Bigger Brain

versus

Stealth Techniques

THE SUBJECT AT hand is the building of stealth defences - with respect to the safe transfer of meaning between individual human beings. Accordingly, we specify aspects of primary-network concealment; with a view to obtaining absolute security for communicated datum(s) [ref. Absolute Security:TARGET and METHOD(S)].[22]

A second goal of this chapter is to define and classify covert mechanism(s) for primary-network defence - by means of logically consistent definitions, analysis and exposition.

---

[22] The OED (2nd Edition) defines 'stealth' thusly: 1) The action or practice of stealing or taking secretly and wrongfully; theft. 2) Contrasted with force or violence. 3) The action of stealing or going furtively into or out of a place; the action of stealing or gliding along unperceived. 4) Furtive or underhand action, an act accomplished by eluding observation or discovery.

Unfortunately, even a single hacked entry-method or exploited attack-surface - can lead to a data-breach that effectively invalidates all the other protective mechanisms. An attacker has to be successful just once (in relation to any number of attacks); whereas a defender must successfully protect datum(s) for each and every attack, or maintain a 100 percent success rate - forever!

A secure system is one that does what it is supposed to. — Eugene Spafford

Zero Day Vulnerability - A zero day vulnerability refers to a hole in software that is unknown to the vendor. This security hole is then exploited by hackers before the vendor becomes aware and hurries to fix it—this exploit is called a **zero day attack**.

Evasion Attack(s)

In network security, **evasion** is bypassing network security in order to deliver an exploit, attack, or other form of malware to a target network or system, without detection.
The security systems are rendered ineffective against well-designed evasion techniques, in the same way that a stealth fighter can attack without detection by radar.

Stealth Defence(s)

A nice antipodal proposition - and remedy for - an evasive attack - is a **stealth defence**. Whereby all physical and virtual system gateways are rendered invisible and/or out-of-reach of the data-processing actions of any harmful attacker(s).

Gateway Protection

A good rule-of-thumb for achieving - socially secure communication - is that it is always easier (and more effective) to eliminate / conceal a system gateway than to protect access to the same gateway. Ergo absolute security involves excluding / disguising entry-point(s) and entry-method(s) for unsafe-actors on the primary-network's data-processing stack.

Storage and Transfer Media

Sometimes, in order to achieve a primary-network design that provides **absolute security** - it may prove advantageous - to disentangle / separate - **transfer** from **storage** functionality. Such an approach can reduce the number of attack-surfaces and/or copies (i.e central copies) that are exposed to attack - and thus render the probability of a successful data-breech far less likely (i.e by moving to a P2P network design). It is important to realise that **socially secure communication** does not (necessarily) include back-up function(s). **Single-copy-send** is not multiple-copy-send - and does not require the creation of central storage / backup-copies. For absolute security, it may be best to let the sender / receiver take care of any and all backup function(s) for themselves - and in terms of creating their own data/account backup(s) - locally (i.e on a PC) - and/or by means of organisational backups etc.

In the present chapter we are concerned with how best to protect form based attack-surface(s); consisting of *physical-gateways* - media of storage, transfer and access; and *virtual-gateways* - formatted copies for storage, transfer and access. Patently - a wide range of - defensive techniques are possible - to protect gateway type(s); and because systems of communication are many and varied. Ergo, it is difficult to identify any universally applicable defensive procedures - without precedence. Nevertheless, we can outline key principles for *primary-network concealment* - the same being methods that may prove useful to the designer of a system that seeks to provide absolute security.

Effective stealth techniques (for defense) - include:

[A] **BLOCK**: Move access-node(s) - plus related data-set(s) - including user data (i.e. **user owned IDs / keys**) - to a private (possibly portable) access-device; closing physical / virtual gateway(s).

[B] **RESTRICT**: Employ an **invitation-only-network + cypher-matching** - whereby unsafe parties are blocked (i.e use a private network).

Public Communication Channel(s)

By definition, any and all data packets flowing along public communication channel(s) / pipeline(s) - existing on an open-network - or the Internet - **ARE - IN SOME ASPECT - PUBLIC**. This is because data-packets must be routed along public data channel(s) - and using known IP and/or HTTP protocols etc. Hence all private-datums, no matter how they are represented - pass along the public information-highway. Ergo, and patently, secure communication involves 'squashing' private datum-copies into public datagrams.

[C] **DECEPTION:** Use false / null data-traffic, decoys, honey-pots, spoofed access-device IP / MAC addresses (hide source + destination IDs/point(s)); hide message(s) in innocuous content; closing invalid gateway(s).

[D] **SECRECY**: Use a secret / scrambled / coded protocol (key-protected); secret routers/gateways - to close / protect all datum physical / virtual-gateway(s).

[E] **CURTAIL:** Eliminate all legitimate and illegitimate secondary copies (e.g. use a Peer-to-Peer (P2P) network); closing physical + virtual gateway(s).

[F] **DEFEND:** Protect the communication channel (e.g. use distributed transport and/or concealed packet(s)).

[G] **CONCEAL:** the method(s) of coding within a large range of possible method(s) + vary / overlap method(s); that is protect meaning gateway(s) (i.e. exploit the beholder's share).

[H] **LOCALISE:** Identity and Access Management System(s). Do not trust private items to nth-parties.

[I] **CONFUSE:** Employ nested protective layers.

In a nutshell, we wish to reduce gateway: exposure (limit existence in place / time), number(s), visibility and fragility - eliminating / nullifying attack-vectors.

By definition, a **defence-method** is a mechanism that prevents unauthorised parties (i.e. unsafe-actors) from gaining entry to one or more system gateway(s). Patently, the designer wishes to minimise the chances of a data-breech - and he/she does so by: A) protecting gateways; and B) reducing gateway: A) numbers, B) potential access location(s), C) time/exposure windows, and D) entry pathway types / numbers.

The title of the present chapter - *Bigger Brain versus Stealth Techniques'* - refers to what we regard as best-practice for building an - absolutely secure - point-to-point system for private communication of meaning. Put simply, we believe that it is far better to rely on stealth techniques - in order to *block (eliminate) / conceal* system gateway(s) - than attempt to have a ***bigger brain*** than all attackers (i.e use ***unbreakable locks***). Remember that for a central-server network; the primary, secondary, tertiary copies etc; hang around effectively <u>forever</u>.

Undertaking to build an unbreakable encryption defence and/or coding method for such (effectively immortal) copies; may be unrealistic. Ergo, attaining robust meaning gateway(s) - is predicated upon - maintenance of superior intelligence / know-how (perpetually) - and because the defence mechanism(s) must stay (at least) one step ahead of all attacker(s) - now and at all times in the future.

A preferable approach - and one that will prove to be - in all likelihood - far less vulnerable to a data-breach; is to move system gateways - beyond the reach of any attackers. Primary-network concealment can be achieved using fundamental techniques that do not rely on having a bigger brain (so-to-speak). Rather we employ carefully chosen hardware and software tools as described - for example - in the list above.

A **system gateway** provides a way to access private datum-copies that exist on the primary-network's data-processing stack (legitimate entry or not).
A gateway provides an access pathway for a copy - potentially bypassing any unrelated entry-defences that may exist for the system as a whole.

Semagram - A form of steganography, wherein encryptions are made of arrangements of objects, images, or symbols rather than by letters or numbers.

An nice stealth defensive mechanism is to limit attack-surface exposure(s) to very short timescales - providing only fleeting visibility to unsafe actors. For example sending datum-copies from one portable USB key-drive to another, whilst using a P2P network (i.e. limited access-node exposure and no central copy exposure).

Gateway Architecture

As previously defined, an **access-gateway** consists of one or more access-nodes and/or exposed attack-surfaces for a primary, secondary or tertiary copy. Earlier in chapter 5 we characterised 3 different types of access-gateway for datum-copies existing on a point-to-point communication system. Firstly, we have **physical-gateway(s)** - which determine who may obtain a physical copy; next we have **virtual-gateway(s)** - which determine who can open a virtual / formatted copy; and finally we have **meaning-gateway(s)** that determine who can decode a copy. To be successful an intruder must (typically) pass through several physical and virtual gateway(s); before decoding all meaning gateway(s) - and in order to uncover the communicated datum(s). Ergo gateway defence-method(s) and/or entry-barriers - typically provide a hierarchy of defensive 'high-walls' - much like a castle (**defence-in-depth**).

Obviously, for absolute security [ref. Absolute Security: TARGET + METHOD(S)], it is best to employ as many nested gateway defences as possible - and in order to maximise the number and depth of defensive mechanism(s) present. However, as stated, it is normally best practice to render (as many as possible) access-gateways - invisible and/or out-of-reach for unwarranted actor(s). Ergo, primary-network entry-method blocking / concealment would seem to be the best approach for defending a communication pipeline; combined with elimination of any unnecessary secondary copies - plus protection of tertiary copies.

FEUDAL SECURITY

With the prevalence of cloud services and locked-down user devices, we're entering a world where IT security is very reminiscent of feudalism. We pledge allegiance to companies like Apple or Google, and in return they promise to protect us. We have little or no control over the security of our iPad, or Gmail accounts, or Facebook data, or Flickr photos; we simply have to trust our feudal lords. Of course, these lords don't always have our best interests at heart, and can easily take advantage of us," said Bruce Schneier author of 'Liars and Outliers'.

We can conclude that the techniques of absolute security are not rocket science - but they are a little unusual in that they do require specialist tools; including potentially: *Peer-to-Peer (P2P) network design, stealth and depth-defences, well-designed encryption / coding, plus localised - or P2P - user ID / key management system(s), user-owned passwords, secret-keys etc.*

Let us now go back to the original purpose of this book. Remember that we had made a distinction between partial / absent and absolute security [ref. Absolute Security: TARGET]. Perhaps for most situations it is fine to have a small degree of additional security provided by a standard encryption method (e.g. using email with a single-layer of encryption). But for those occasions when one has to communicate datum(s) that are of a particularly high value (i.e. be ***private-by-guarantee***) - then we must employ special techniques.

Unfortunately, attaining absolute security is challenging using standard (central-server) tools such as email and file-sharing systems like **DropBox, GoogleDrive** etc; because - as we have seen - these systems are open to a host of exploits, intercepts and data-breaches. Such problems relate to structural vulnerabilities in terms of network design (i.e. long-term exposure of physical gateways); leaving only virtual and meaning gateway protective techniques.

Private by Guarantee

Privacy can be defined as **socially restricted access** for an item, and it is a status that must be upheld/defended by some protective methods (i.e specific accessibility pathways in terms of who may see, know and/or change the item). **Private-by-guarantee** means that there is no possibility of the item's privacy status being changed - at any place/time - and under any circumstances whatsoever.

In summary, attaining absolute security for our digital communication(s) - is a difficult-to-reach - but not impossible - goal. Just like the magician, rather than performing any real magic tricks (achieving unbreakable encryption / coding) - we misdirect.

Accordingly,

we seek to:

(A) **Lock / block / conceal system gateway(s);**

(B) **Conceal the method(s) of entry / defence (variable aspects)** within a large range - of (potential) methods;

(C) Employ **depth-defences** to confuse / slow-down an attacker.

In this manner,

we safeguard attack-surface entry-methods.

Coded Transmission(s) versus Coded Meaning(s)

By definition, a datagram exists - on a networked system - in the form of a hierarchy of coded layers. Whereby the process of transferring a group of related datum-copies (for example letters in a text-file) from one IP node to another; requires that lower level binary bits are used to assemble higher level packetised structures - which in turn create individual ASCI letters. This is an example of **Coded Transmission(s)** - or the use of public codes to facilitate data transfer(s). Such code types are sharply distinguished from the **Coding of Meaning** - whereby secret codes are used to mask and/or conceal the meaning of communicated symbols - and by means of unusual symbol-meaning mapping(s) etc.

Chapter Nine

Privacy and Security:

The Big Picture

THE SUBJECT AT hand is the safe transfer of meaning between individual human beings. Accordingly, we specify key principles of design for a nominal primary-network; and with a view to obtaining absolute security for communicated datum(s) [ref. Absolute Security: TARGET)].

A second goal of this chapter is to define and classify safe mechanism(s) for primary-network defence - by means of logically consistent definitions, analysis and exposition.[23]

---

[23] In a nutshell, we can characterise a private / secure communication system as being concerned with: A) **Locking / Blocking / Concealing: Physical / Virtual System Gateway(s)**; B) **Providing sufficiently secure Identity and Access Management mechanism(s)** - including properly secure secret-keys / unlocking mechanism(s) / logins & passwords etc; and C) **Protecting - or Locking - Meaning Gateways** by means of sufficiently robust encryption and coding mechanism(s).

N.B. Concealment / camouflaging of a system access gateway - is a one-time technique (for an individual gateway), hence you cannot reanimate it after the first failure - as opposed to key expiration whereby you simply throw it away and get a new one.

We posit that the well-known Shannon's / Kerckhoffs's principle has been misinterpreted to drive the security community away from deception/stealth-based security systems / methods / mechanisms (See page 40 and note below).

Usability

In human-computer interaction - **usability** - studies the elegance and clarity with which the interaction with a computer program is designed; but usability also considers usefulness.

Privacy and Security

Doubtless it is quite possible for two humans to communicate with privacy and absolute security - and by means of a 'self-assembled' set of special language(s)/code(s) plus a Peer-to-Peer (P2P) network etc. But the question of usability is raised - or how practical is it to transfer messages, files and folders etc; using the chosen tools. Is the process difficult and/or time-consuming?

Secrecy vs Stealth

Generally, information-security designs that work well - do not rely on being kept secret (i.e. in terms of using **secret form(s)** for algorithm(s) / method). Hence, Shannon's maxim: 'assume that the enemy knows the system' (see note on bottom of page). However **stealth defence(s)** - or concealment / camouflaging of system access gateways - may still be a valid technique.

N.B. We consider that Shannon's maxim: 'assume the enemy knows the system' refers purely to aspects of an entry/defence-method's **form** alone (i.e conceptual form/design of the locking/blocking/concealing entry/defence mechanism(s)). Whereas aspects of the **instantiation** of the employed **secure entry/defence-method(s)** (i.e. secret-keys / coding variables / particular access-device location(s) / node login details) - may obviously remain secret. And because this is what security is - protection of privacy by means of restricted/robust **entry/defence-method(s)** - system elements that cannot be fraudulently discovered/used/over-run; or defences that are inaccessible to unsafe-actors. However it may be that Shannon meant to say that a defender should avoid - relying upon secrecy by means of identical locking/blocking/concealing techniques (i.e the same **form(s)**) - over-and-over again - and because they may (or certainly will) be discovered. Ergo, one can still rely on **secrecy** of an entry/defence-method's **form** - **if it changes often enough** - and without (necessarily) compromising security in any way.

Over the past 8 chapters, we have developed a new top-level theory of secure point-to-point system(s) for private communication of meaning. Along the way, we identified - a logically consistent - set of terms, principles and recommendations; with which to characterise and compare-and-contrast the different system types. Largely, implementation details have been cast aside - but (hopefully) not at the expense of lucidity, rigour and/or truthful analysis.

Space limitations have precluded any - detailed analysis of - *Identity / Access / Secret-Key Management System(s)* - however these topics have been well-examined elsewhere - and in lower-level treatment(s). In any case, we are now in position to ask: what does an ideal system look like - what are its specific features - and how can we deliver *absolute security?*

Ofttimes manufacturers put forward the view that a particular networked system is immune to hacking / spying as a result of this fact - or for that pre-eminent reason - and/or simply because it uses that method etc. But if there is a key lesson of the cybersecurity field - it has been that no single defensive technique is a source of ultimate safety - rather it is the *whole system that must be secure, by design, implementation and operation.*

The Cyber Ripple Theory

...states that "the effect of a cyber attack on an organisation or individual has a destructive cascading effect both on the connecting technology and the human aspects that are linked. Further the extend of the destruction depends on the awareness and protection levels around the sequential points of the attack." - Professor Richard Benham - May 2014

Latest Security Mantra
Don't trust anything from the US
government (ref. Snowden / Assange et al).

Skepticism

Today's systems must anticipate future attacks. Any comprehensive system — whether for authenticated communications, secure data storage, or electronic commerce — is likely to remain in use for five years or more. It must be able to withstand the future: smarter attackers, more computational power, and greater incentives to subvert a widespread system. There won't be time to upgrade it in the field.

It is prudent to apply skepticism in response to any forthright claims of impregnability when it comes to a (standardised) digital communication system. In light of recent events (NSA spying & Edward Snowden etc), it has become clear that conventional systems are far less secure than most people had realised. Ergo, we can no longer listen to the security promises / guarantees of some rather narrow cybersecurity 'experts' - without a certain degree of scepticism; and because countless data-breeches indicate that (at least some) people were either lying, deceptive or just plain wrong.

Accordingly, we need to know what has gone wrong with security systems - on a world-wide basis - because everyday we see new instances of stolen, lost and compromised data - and on systems that were supposed to be impregnable. We need a new open language of security vulnerability, plus assessment methods to judge one system against another. We might also ask - who is designing our technologies - and why? Have we been lied-to / deceived? If so, what can we do about it - and how?

Incredibly, some security 'experts' do not ever connect their personal computers to the Internet! It is as if they had given up - and believe that nothing (no security defence) offered even the slightest chance of protection. Most people are not so lucky as the same 'experts' who can simply disconnect from the Internet - and then run around giving everyone else (somewhat contradictory) advice.

Information Security Indicators

Benchmarking of computer security requires measurements for comparing both different IT systems and single IT systems. The technical approach is a pre-defined catalog of security events (security incident and vulnerability (computing)) together with corresponding formula for the calculation of security indicators that are accepted and comprehensive. **Information Security Indicators** have been standardised by the ETSI Industrial Specification Group (ISG) ISI. These indicators provide the basis to switch from a qualitative to a quantitative culture in IT Security Scope of measurements: External and internal threats (attempt and success), user's deviant behaviours, nonconformities and/or vulnerabilities (software, configuration, behavioural, general security framework). The **European Telecommunications Standards Institute (ETSI)** is an independent, not-for-profit, standardisation organisation in the telecommunications industry.

Patently, the designer does not (and cannot) know what will be the precise user-case scenario(s) - or specific nature(s) of the complex technological environment(s) - in which a particular communication system will be used.

Hence what can be done?

In a nutshell, it is my belief that we must - fight for the right - to recognise, know and comprehend what are the underlying principles - plus assumptions - used in each case. Accordingly, we need an open, valid - all-encompassing - *theory of information security* - and primarily to define what it actually means (*logically*, *philosophically* and *socially*) to keep information safe.

Ergo, and by means of this book, we henceforth submit a new (unified) theory of absolute security.[24]

---

[24] In his famous paper 'Communication Theory of Secrecy Systems', Dr Claude Shannon made a distinction between three types of secrecy as follows: A) **Concealment Systems** - in which the existence of the message is concealed from the enemy - or in our terms physical/virtual/meaning gateway concealment (finding action(s) are blocked); and B) **Privacy Systems** - which use special equipment to recover the message (i.e. transfer/access/storage - and (for example) physical/virtual gateway blocking (form entry pathway action(s) blocked)); and C) **'True' Secrecy Systems** - whereby the meaning of the message is concealed by cipher / code etc; (i.e. metrical, descriptive and selectional attack-surfaces are protected (content entry action(s) are locked)). In his paper Shannon explored (rigorously) only the 3rd type - whereas in this short book we have - at least superficially - analysed all 3 types. Ergo, we have identified 3 different gateways types - physical / virtual / meaning; plus 3 classes of attack surface(s) that may exist within a specific meaning gateway.

The problem most organisations will have with proper security is that it is complex to administer, can be hard to use, expensive and typically requires specialised, disciplined people and tech. Security policy must also be valued   and adhered to by the rest of the organisation's stakeholders.

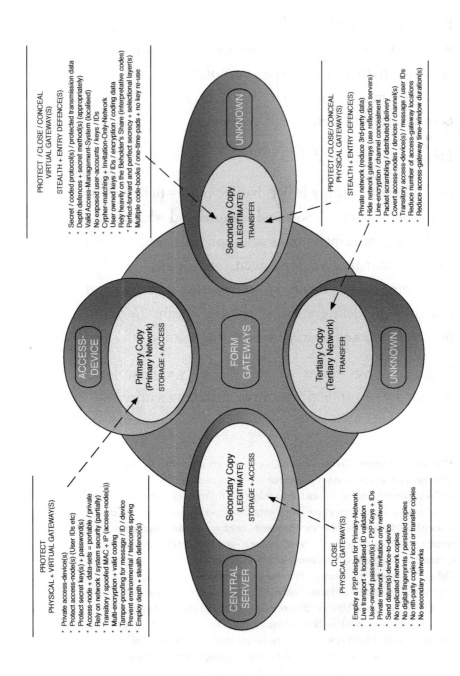

Figure 6,7,8 (left and right pages): Primary, Secondary and Tertiary

Network(s) - MEANING AND FORM Gateway(s)

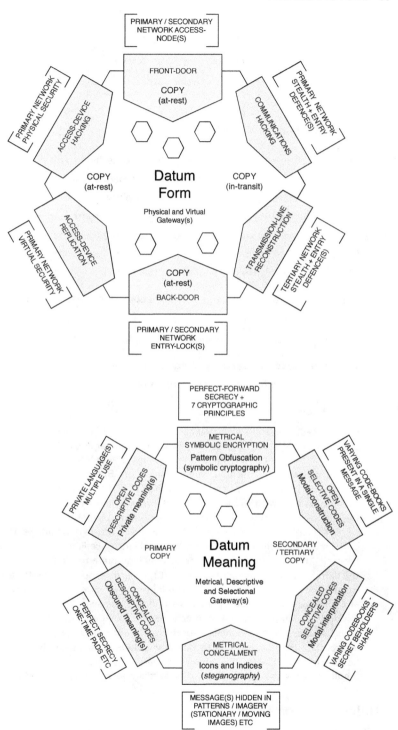

Cyberwarfare specialists cautioned this week that the Internet was effectively a "wilderness of mirrors," and that attributing the source of cyberattacks and other kinds of exploitation is difficult at best and sometimes impossible. Despite the initial assertions and rumors that North Korea was behind the attacks and slight evidence that the programmer had some familiarity with South Korean software, the consensus of most computer security specialists is that the attackers could be located anywhere in the world. — John Markoff

Theory / System

Theory: A conception or mental scheme of something to be done, or of the method of doing it; a systematic statement of rules or principles to be followed. **Logic**: The branch of philosophy concerned with the use and study of valid reasoning. Among the important properties of logical systems are: **consistency** (no contradictory theorems), **validity** (no false inferences), **completeness** (true and provable formulae), and **soundness** (premises are true in the actual world).

System: A set or assemblage of things connected, associated, or interdependent, so as to form a complex unity; a whole composed of parts in orderly arrangement according to some scheme or plan.

Theory of Absolute Security = logical scheme and/or prescribed system for providing socially secure communication.[25]

------

[25] How might we best summarise and/or develop - optimistically - a philosophy of **Absolute Security**? Perhaps we can begin by stating that: A) for two parties to communicate a message (i.e. datum(s)) privately and with guaranteed security; and by means of: B) a communication channel that is in some sense 'public'; then C) it is a basic premise that the two parties must (by some method) protect (lock / block / conceal) the message content(s) from access by other (unwarranted) parties; and D) that the protection is performed by means of **wholly/partially secret entry-method(s)** (including the locking/blocking/concealing of accessibility action(s)) - which enables only legitimate parties to unlock the communicated meaning; whereby: E) the **protected entry-method(s)** must remain (at least partially) private (in terms of form and/or content); and F) typically the **protected entry-method(s)** consist of some private 'locking/blocking/concealment' mechanism(s) / key(s) / algorithm(s) / physical-device(s) / transmission-protocol(s) / entry-paths / interpretive-method(s) etc. N.B. Ultimately, **there is no alternative** to the holding (by both parties - or sender/receiver) - of one-or-more - shared **wholly secret entry-method(s)** and/or **partially secret entry-method(s)**.

N.B. Use of term Secret

In footnote 23 (plus the note on page 58), **secret** refers to a socially restricted entry-method that is known/usable only by the sender and receiver parties.

Chapter Ten

A Theory of
Absolute Security

OUR GOAL HAS been to characterise a *communication system* for replicating information patterns - encapsulated as discrete units of data (messages / files / folders) - between remote computer nodes; whilst preserving the social integrity (privacy) of said patterns in place and time. A second goal was to define safe mechanism(s) for primary-network defence - by means of logically consistent definitions, analysis and exposition.

Overall, and along-the-way - we have specified a new *theory of absolute security.* This same theory provides a unified set of concepts and first-principles; and hence design guidelines - with which to define / provide: *socially secure communication*. Accordingly, I leave it to the reader to appraise the extent to which the aforementioned goals have been met; and to adjudge the validity / usefulness of the proposed - theory of absolute security.

In the OED, **Absolute** is define thusly: 1) Detached, disengaged, unfettered. 2) Absolved, loosened, detached, disengaged (from). 3a) Disengaged from all accidental or special circumstances; essential, general. 3b) Absolute in quality or degree; perfect. 4a) Free from all imperfection or deficiency; complete, finished; perfect, consummate. 4b) Originally: absolved, disengaged: then adj. disengaged or free from imperfection or qualification; from interference, connexion, relation, comparison, dependence; from condition etc. See Appendix M for our definition of absolute in the context of security.

A concise work on 'password-strength' has been given in 'A Canonical Password Strength Measure' - by Eugene Panferov (http://arxiv.org/abs/1505.05090)

It used to be expensive to make things public and cheap to make them private. Now it's expensive to make things private and cheap to make them public. — Clay Shirky

British Standard 7799: A standard code of practice and provides guidance on how to secure an information system. It includes the management framework, objectives, and control requirements for information security management systems.

Information-Security Crisis

It is interesting to note that a good deal of disagreement exists amongst the experts - as to which point-to-point communication system, if any, is fully secure. For example, practitioners have long argued over symmetric (local private shared key) and asymmetric (PGP) encryption - with proponents from both sides claiming that the other's methods are inherently are more vulnerable. What we can say with certainty is that neither side is correct - and that both methods have drawbacks - depending upon the specific features of a particular user-case scenario.

According to recent press revelations, a variety of back-doors have been built into standard encryption methods. For example, random number generators have been deliberately altered to make them - less than random. Ergo, all dependent ciphers are rendered somewhat less than secure (regardless of user passwords etc).

It is now commonplace to hear of numerous other systematic data-breaches and encryption-related problems (i.e. deliberate and/or accidental vulnerabilities). It is obvious that the information-security field is in crisis. Accordingly, we must now **re-evaluate the entire field of information-security** - and re-examine its founding principles and core assumptions. At the same time, we must impel system designers to work on more effective solutions for information-security. We put a man on the <u>moon</u> - surely it is not beyond the ken of humans to make secure and private communication possible - and for everyone / everywhere.

Password Entry Systems employ a **password** - which is a word or string of characters used for user authentication to prove identity or access approval to gain access to a resource (example: an access code is a type of password), which should be kept secret from those not allowed access.Despite the name, there is no need for passwords to be actual words; indeed passwords which are not actual words may be harder to guess, a desirable property. The terms **passcode** and **passkey** are sometimes used when the secret information is purely numeric, such as the personal identification number (PIN) commonly used for ATM access.

Doubtless, it is a truism that sometimes one cannot see the **wood-for-the-trees** in terms of identifying the precise relationships between the technical (structural) aspects of how a system works and its varied - and perhaps unpredictable (functional) influences on the wider *human world*. A blindspot may exist in terms of understanding how a system operates to produce certain functional outcomes. Sometimes (or often) we do not have a full understanding of how - or why - a system works structurally; and due to factors such as the *diversity, complexity* and the *partial invisibility* of operational situation(s), plus due to the presence of hidden / unpredictable influencing factors and/or unknown / arbitrary low-level design features etc.

But if any blindspot(s) also exist for the designers / operators, then it may be that we are all in very serious trouble, because it would appear that nobody knows - or can begin to explain - what may be the functional effect(s) of our systems, computers and machines.

Accordingly, we (the users) must be able to understand (at the very least) what are the operating principles / assumptions for our communication technologies; and in particular *how, when, where* and *why*; they interrelate with wider **social workflows** to form everyday communication systems.

Two Factor Authentication, also known as 2FA, two step verification or TFA (as an acronym), is an extra layer of security that is known as "multi factor authentication" that requires not only a password and username but also something that only the user has on them, i.e. a (second) piece of information that only they possess. Often 2FA/TFA can usefully employ something only the user can physically display (e.g. finger-prints, retina pattern) - in order to enhance security protection.

But in terms of present-day systems, this is precisely what we often do <u>not</u> have - knowledge of the ways in which our systems may (possibly) fail to live up to our expectations. In other words - in this book - we uphold **open-security** - not-so-much in terms of specific security method(s) - but rather for top-level design principle(s). It has been our position that for - information-security - missing are **axiomatic principles** - or founding definitions / propositions related to the 'human-side' of the equation. Consequently, we have endeavoured to bring **unity, clarity** and **logical structure** - or holism - to the topic of socially secure communication.

I need hardly remind the reader of the very real problem(s) facing anyone who wished to obtain certainty in relation to protecting the privacy of his / her digital communications. Many people believe that **absolute security** is, quite simply, impossible to achieve. Why should this be the case? And why is there a widespread belief that - it is somehow inevitable - that current systems must be fundamentally insecure? Patently, the answer relates (partly) to the countless data-breaches that occur on a daily basis. And astoundingly, it seems that the very same people who advised us on cybersecurity - the world's top experts - have actually helped the NSA build encryption back-doors into vast numbers of *computers, phones* and *networked communication devices*.

On the need for private-thoughts / ideas / datum(s): Why do we have thoughts in any case; fundamentally because they are for personal and private use; what is the alternative—automatons who are told what to think, say and do?

Unfortunately however, these same back-door(s) are available to hackers. Nevertheless, perhaps the NSA have done us all a favour - by (inadvertently) exposing an industry - information-security - that is rampant with false-promises and undelivered guarantees. Professor Phillip Rogaway has recently written an article entitled *'The Moral Failure of Computer Scientists'* - in relation to this issue (2016).

What can be done to bring belief / trustworthiness - back to the field of information-security?

Perhaps we can begin by asking: what is the nature of private communication? In this respect - we offer up a quick hint - by suggesting that privacy and security (for interpersonal communication(s)) - may be ***fundamental human right(s)***. I know that related issue(s) are contentious - and much debated - but surely we (as a people) should at least consider the implications of the **United Nations Declaration of Human Rights** - with respect to the free exchange of ideas (i.e. protection of open / private / secret-thoughts).

We might even consider creating an ***information-security declaration of human rights (or techno-rights)*** - in terms of the provision of founding principles - for computer, system and machine design(s).

In his book **The Future of Human Rights**, human ethics Professor Upendra Baxi, says that human rights languages, however effete remain perhaps all that we have to interrogate the barbarism of power. Baxi says: human rights are the best hope there is for a participative making, and re-making of human futures.

N.B. Info-Sec is such a vastly complex - and rapidly evolving - technological field - that it is impossible to depict anything but a rudimentary facsimile (of a small sub-region) of the same in a single book. Nevertheless, holism is the key goal.

N.B. The **theory of absolute security** outlined here - whilst striving to be complete in terms of founding principles and fundamental definitions etc; must (obviously) be seen as work in progress (for the security community as a whole).

Placing such (utopian?) ideas aside, we must acknowledge that networked communication system(s) exist in a dangerous - and unlawful - environment that is analogous to the wild-west.

Whereby countless unsafe-actors represent real danger(s) to communicated private-datum(s).

What to do?

Well (at a minimum) we need full disclosure / agreement - and in relation to valid founding principles for truly effective communication tools. Evidently, it is necessary to bring the computer back to an original and primary purpose - interpersonal communication without spies / hacks / dangers. In summary, we must impel designers to work on more effective solutions when it comes to information-security; using rational / ethical principles based on logically consistent - and publicly visible / critique-able - definitions, concepts and theories.

Ergo, my hope is that - the *theory of absolute security* - introduced here - can prove useful for application to future point-to-point system(s) for private communication of meaning.

Breaking encryption with brute force is all about time and resources. The more time and resources an attacker must devote to their attack, the harder it is for them to succeed. The added "strength" of two layers is that it is already difficult to break one layer of encryption, so breaking two layers will be even more difficult. Remember that encryption is just one (important) link in the security chain. If we apply the "inner fortress" principle, the very hardest encryption or defence layers will be on the inside. The assumption is that attackers are more easily detected (or worn out) as they attempt to penetrate increasingly difficult security perimeters. Medieval castles were built on similar principles as are most secure installations. First the moats, pikes and outer walls, then the hot pitch and finally the fortified, elevated keep.

Chapter Eleven

Real Life

Scenarios

A S WE BRING this short book on *Absolute Security* to a close; it seems appropriate to reflect on our findings. That is, to examine - or match - prescribed-theory with real-world security concerns.

Desired is security for all our digital communications.

Earlier we defined absolute security as ***socially secure communication*** - or ***single-copy-send*** - for a private-datum; in terms of safely transferring datum(s) from sender to receiver. We adopted a duel 'zoomed-in' plus 'wide-angled' perspective on privacy. Along the way we have - carefully mapped - key characteristics of privacy / security - and (hopefully) by means of insightful analysis plus suitable terminology for attendant processes. Q.E.D.

But where are we now? Theory is - all very well and good - but it must have purpose. Unfortunately, several questions remain; such as: A) *what precisely is absolute security (in real-world terms); and B) how is it obtained; and even C) <u>can</u> it be obtained?*

Earlier we pinned down *absolute security* thusly...

Absolute security - for a point-to-point communication system - is the replication of a single instance (or primary-copy) of a datum from one socially restricted access-node to another [ref. Absolute Security: TARGET]. In other words, it is the **single-copy-send** of a datum from one party to another; whereby no - socially accessible - nth-party copies exist whatsoever (hopefully persistently)... thus ... [Absolute Security[and [Partial / Absent Security] are binary dualisms - or mutually exclusive true/false values for any act of communication.

Hence absolute security is protection of ***privacy-status*** for a datum-copy. Ergo, it relates to the maintenance of social accessibility restriction(s) for private-datum(s). Whereby we achieve single-copy-send - now and (hopefully) at all times in the future. Accordingly, absolute security can be thought of as an objective true/false value, in and of itself. Hence an item either: ***is absolutely secure*** - or else: ***it is not absolutely secure*** - at any specific epoch - and for a particular environment / communication instance.

As stated, the absolute security TARGET is defined as single-copy-send for the encapsulated meaning (i.e certainty of protection). But it may be that at some post-communication epoch: *A) the system / data is successfully hacked - and datum(s) are exposed to unsafe-actors; and hence B) the judgement of secure communication was / is / will-become false.*

And best practice security procedures, process and constant vigilance are equally vital, because the security boundaries, vulnerabilities and goal posts will always be shifting. If you don't keep repairing and fortifying the castle walls or fail to keep an eye out for the latest marauders, eventually you will fall.

Consequently, privacy status may change; and security is patently a situation-specific / time-dependant quality. As a result, it seems clear that absolute security must be - in one sense - a purely *objective property*. However because it is influenced by perceptions / judgements / predictions - it is at the same time a *subjective property*.

Evidently, factors such as: *inadequate knowledge of any/all unsafe-actors; plus hidden and changing threat types* - can cause incorrect and/or revised predictions in this respect. Henceforth making judgment(s) - as to the various *capability*, *coverage* and *control* aspects of security is especially difficult - because these are inevitably human assessed factors (automatic monitoring / reporting systems aside).

Absolute security status is simultaneously a *goal, metric, judgment and prediction;* in addition to being an ostensive fact/truth. Accordingly, many interrelating factors are evident for a particular system operating at any specific epoch. At the very least - the person making the cybersecurity judgment(s) / decision(s) seeks to:

A) Be in possession of all the facts - or make accurate predictions on real-world: threats / defensive capabilities, and judge the effectiveness of threat-models; plus accuracy of monitoring system(s) etc; and

B) Adequately perceive/understand labyrinthine relationship(s) between multiple, complex, fixed and/or changing factors for relevant: systems / tools / networks / actors / attackers etc - including future ones; and

C) Implement valid cybersecurity measures, plus avoid / correct mistakes etc.

> You have to ask yourself two questions: first, is there any chance that we can be more secure than a company that specialises in technology and knows that information security is core to its very existence? And second, who would really give a damn about what we hold on our disks anyway?

The defender seeks to accurately: *perceive, measure and understand* all relevant factors; and so to assess which ones will influence overall cybersecurity strategy. Ergo privacy status may be partly a **perception, model, prediction, belief** and/or **truth / falsehood**; depending upon your point of view and information / knowledge level(s).

Ultimately cybersecurity involves assimilation of intelligence from as many as possible of the different: *threats, actors, entry and defensive methods present.* Hence cybersecurity is an interdependent capability - and it must be constantly monitored and defended; plus - be ever adapting to the changing needs / requirements of the open-network's perilous environment. Unfortunately, the real-life situation may be even worse than this, because whenever you share access to a digital item - you trust: A) any and all primary / secondary **network users** (i.e. *multiple humans*); plus; B) the **communication-system** itself (i.e. primary and secondary network security). Ergo, dangers may include both human and systematic vulnerabilities.

Earlier, we defined unauthorised datum-copy access (generally) - as an ordered series of goals - or a path - to be navigated. In real-world terms - any attacker desires the capability to **see/touch/open** a datum-copy's form and/or content. Attendant accessibility actions are **finding, contacting** and **knowing** a datum's meaning. Q.E.D.

A pressing concern for many is the extra operational challenge of on-premise data storage. To ease the pain, Iron Mountain recommends a tiered information storage approach that defines what is most used, most critical and most confidential, as well as what is dormant, and structuring storage, access and backup accordingly.

Evidently, protecting any item from unsafe-actors - involves first building a defensive wall and/or unbridgeable barrier around it; prior to then providing an entrance-way for authorised parties (which must also be defended).

Whereby, the *finding action* (for a human / programmatic actor and his/her helper actors) is detection of an item's material self (i.e. the datum-copy's form). For example, locating a datum-copy's form existing on a primary, secondary or tertiary network (media of access, storage and/or transfer for a copy). Concordantly, the *contacting* action refers to the full mapping of datum-copy's interior form (true possession of content). Finally, the *knowing action* is the opening-up / reading of meaning for the copy.

Accordingly, protecting access for unsafe-actors normally involves: **concealing** (ref find); **blocking** (ref contacting); and/or **locking** (ref knowing); for datum-copies on the data-processing stack. Henceforth this book has been concerned with techniques to afford protective measures for datum-copies. Unfortunately measuring / quantifying the effectiveness - of any and all of these protective factors - may also be seen as judgments / predictions - in and of themselves. This is because they are (likewise) human-made / fallible entities that must cope with other (perhaps unknown) entities; specifically ones that may have been designed to nullify said anti-discovery / defensive techniques. What to do?

Key protection is a classic case of 'who guards the guards?' It is possible to build key management processes around the idea of a quorum so that more than one administrator is needed to administer keys. Alternatively, you could use local key storage - and remove all n-th parties from the risk register.

Feasibly we can apply a little - deeper theory - and ask what is the nature of protection - or what are the most effective defensive techniques? (i.e. risk-free ones) Evidently there are any number of different types of *concealment defences* - depending upon the specific nature of the entry-method / defence-method one is trying to conceal (see note blow).

For example, we can conceal existence by **masking structure** (in form, location and/or time). Whereby there are three basic processes: A) **conceal by transformation** of form/location/time; or B) **conceal by similarity (equivalency)** - that is by hiding an item alongside a large number (of ostensibly identical) items; and C) **conceal by difference (complexity)** - or hiding an item amongst a large number of greatly/potentially varying forms/structures. Fundamentally the process of masking detection - in this manner - requires just the right amount of concealment; and according to the specific capabilities of the penetration method(s) that are likely to be employed.

Likewise there are different types of **blocking techniques**. We can block a system entrance pathway by eliminating it all-together (for a particular class of unsafe-actor); or else we can employ **navigation complexity** *and/or* **movement barriers** to make the path difficult to traverse. This can be achieved by filling the path with many *false-entrances*, or maze-like pathways etc. An example would be distributed data transport, and/or segmented transfer for datagrams.

Conceal by Decoy: Another way to mask an item's structure is by hiding real content (or meaning) within a layer of apparently ordinary / innocuous content - wherein (for example) you sign off a message with 'Sincerely Yours' - whenever you agree with the message contents, or just 'Regards' - when you do not agree etc.

Finally, it is feasible to lock a system entrance gateway by a means of special: *algorithm(s); watermark(s); facial, retina and finger-print recognition system(s) etc;* and/or other *diversity locks* (i.e. secret patterns, methods, markers, keys etc); combined with *content concealment* through transformation / similarity / difference. And to top-it-all, defences can be overlaid - aka defence-in-depth.

But perhaps we have gone about as far as a general theory can take us - in terms of making all-purpose recommendation(s) about how to protect copies existing on primary, secondary and tertiary networks. We simply do not know enough about the real-world systems in question. In any case, listing all of the potential attack/defence techniques used - would prove exhaustive. By what means then, in a such a short book, can we summarise how the system designer/user should go about protecting a data-processing stack from all possible attacks?

The answer lies in asking and continually re-asking - the right questions - plus challenging assumptions - in relation to cybersecurity. Firstly, we desire to know - *what types of data require which types of protection and why - and for how long*. In the past (prior to Bradley Manning, the Internet etc); military organisations were very good at this type of thing - categorisation of security access levels etc. That is assigning confidentiality / accessibility levels to every item of data - or individual unit of information / knowledge.

Christian Toon, previous head of information risk in Europe for Iron Mountain, (now with PwC) believes companies should "Capture the generation, distribution, accounting, storage, use and destruction of cryptographic keying material and issue a high-level key management policy to guide the business users," he says.

However that was before open-network complexity exploded; and the attackers/attack-vectors multiplied in numbers, types, motivations and capabilities etc. Nevertheless, a good rule-of-thumb - as detailed in chapter 8 - is to consider who needs to have access to the item/system and why. Physical and virtual denial/blocking techniques - to eliminate certain actors - may be the safest way to proceed.

Patently obvious - at the same time - is that we should involve all *partners, stakeholders, and legitimate users* in any cybersecurity analysis or strategy development; plus operation(s). Everyone must be adequately briefed - continually - and on the changing nature of likely threats / responses. When an individual must rely on his/her own capabilities - it becomes difficult to know where to go for advice. Do we trust the cloud providers like Google and Apple - or else look for P2P solutions; or even avoid / abandon the digital-world for our most private items? Finding answers is not so easy - because they depend upon a host of technical, human and situation-specific factors.

It is often easier to make recommendations to people - in relation to cybersecurity - who know a lot about the technical aspects of security; but less-so for less-technical people. This is so partly because less-geeky people (perhaps understandably) have other concerns, and/or they are not interested in all of the (confusing) technical details involved.

"Criminals and states that want to attack organisations can now choose from vast catalogues of pre-made malware", an expert explained, meaning that although the number of attacks is not increasing, they are becoming increasingly sophisticated. "The provision of malware is now big business," another explained. "It comes with the same kind of guarantees that software from Microsoft or one of the other big software houses has." - Business Reporter - 2015 Cyber-Security Summary

Here in this book we have avoided technical details - so far as we were able. The book has charted close-to-the-wind in terms of exploring relationships between a host of *technical and human-centric concepts / principles* (hopefully to useful effect). Overall, we sought to unify the technical and human - opportunities and risks - for information security.

As stated - security is **protection of privacy of meaning.** However the simple logical clarity of this statement changes in certain subtle and difficult to determine ways - when it crosses-over into the realm of cyber. In particular - in the digital-world - nothing is entirely private - and one must lock/block/conceal all illicit entry-methods for private items. As many as possible of the **physical, virtual** and **meaning gateways** must be protected - and in order to retain any chance of achieving absolute security. It is also my opinion, that attaining absolute security - or **assured protection** - in relation to the privacy of our interpersonal communication(s) - is not some impossible dream - mythical being - or paper-tiger. Rather, socially secure communication demands that the communicants abide by a relatively straight-forward set of principles and systemic / technological theory - and employ communication tools that do the same.

Nobody said it would be easy to *communicate privately, safely and with integrity plus assurance*; it isn't; but despite the existence of many dangers / pitfalls, **absolute security** is eminently achievable.

Privacy is not for the passive.

— Jeffrey Rosen

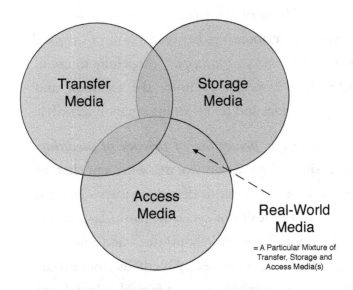

Real-World
Media

= A Particular Mixture of
Transfer, Storage and
Access Media(s)

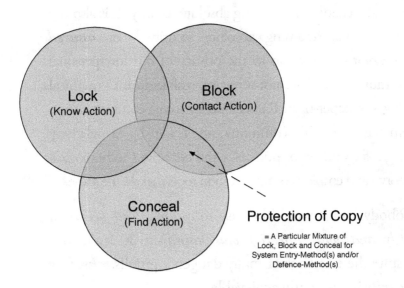

Protection of Copy

= A Particular Mixture of
Lock, Block and Conceal for
System Entry-Method(s) and/or
Defence-Method(s)

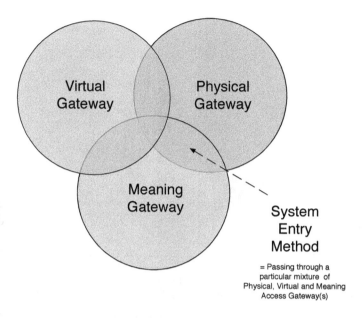

System
Entry
Method

= Passing through a
particular mixture of
Physical, Virtual and Meaning
Access Gateway(s)

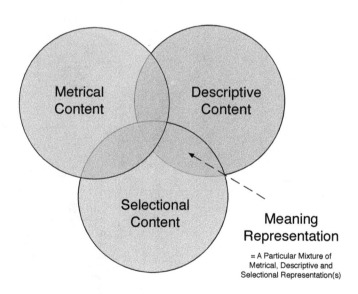

Meaning
Representation

= A Particular Mixture of
Metrical, Descriptive and
Selectional Representation(s)

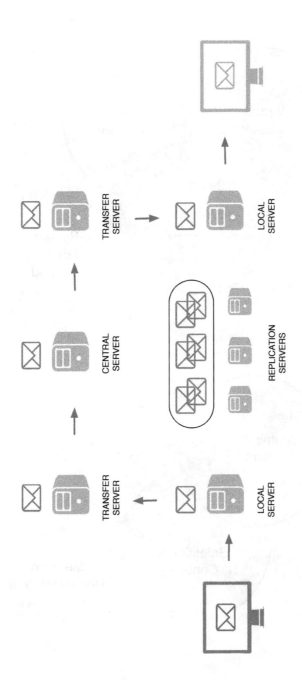

Figure 12: Datum-Copy Transfer on a Central-Server Communication System

Additional Nth Party - Legitimate Secondary Copies (organizational, transfer, replication copies etc); shown as small red envelopes.

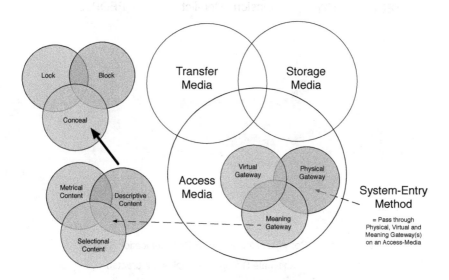

SPHERE OF PROTECTION

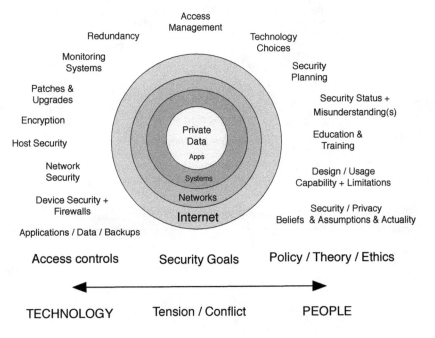

Access
Management

Redundancy

Technology
Choices

Monitoring
Systems

Security
Planning

Patches &
Upgrades

Security Status +
Misunderstanding(s)

Encryption

Host Security

Private
Data

Education &
Training

Apps

Network
Security

Systems

Design / Usage
Capability + Limitations

Networks

Device Security +
Firewalls

Internet

Security / Privacy
Beliefs & Assumptions & Actuality

Applications / Data / Backups

Access controls   Security Goals   Policy / Theory / Ethics

TECHNOLOGY   Tension / Conflict   PEOPLE

REFLECTION
SERVER

Figure 17: Datum-Copy Transfer on a P2P Communication System
No nth-Party - Legitimate Secondary Copies are created.

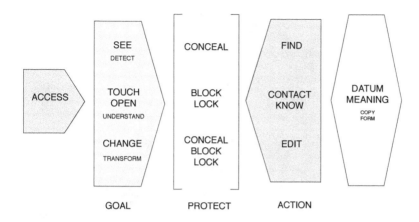

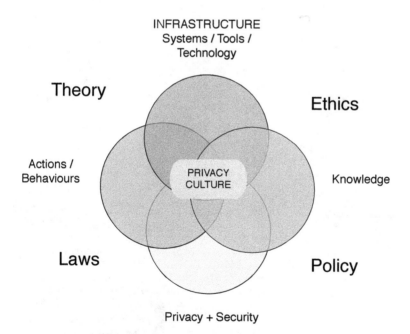

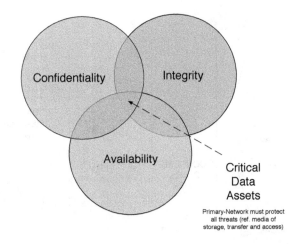

Critical
Data
Assets

Primary-Network must protect
all threats (ref. media of
storage, transfer and access)

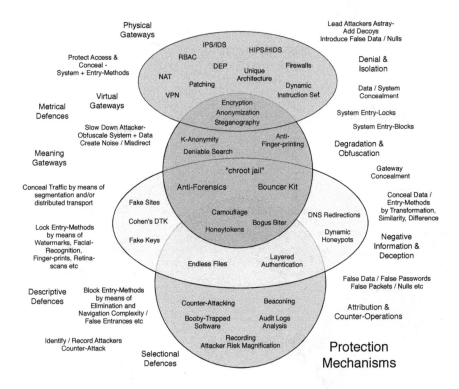

Notes

PREFACE

1. Radley, A.: *Computers as Self.* Fourth International Workshop in Human-Computer Interaction, Tourism and Cultural Heritage in Rome, Italy. (2013)
2. Wiener, N.:*The Human Use of Human Beings.*(1950)
3. Orwell, G.: *Nineteen Eight-Four.* (1949)
4. Foucault, M.: *Discipline and Punishment.* (1975)
5. Russell, Bertrand.: *Skeptical Essays.* (1963)
6. Nelson, T.: *Computer Lib / Dream Machines.* (1974)

INTRODUCTION

1. Levy, S.: *How the NSA nearly destroyed the Internet.* Wired. (January 2014)
2. Veltman, K.: *The Alphabets of Life.* (2014)
3. Lanier, J.: *Who Owns the Future.* (2013)
4. Bush, V.: *As We May Think. The Atlantic.* (1945)
5. Otlet, P.: Monde: *Essai d'universalisme.* (1935)
6. Veltman, K.: *Understanding New Media.* (2006)
7. Gibson, W.: *Neuromancer.* (1984)
8. Berners-Lee, T.: *Weaving the Web.* (1999)
9. Berners-Lee, T.: *World wide Web needs bill of rights.* On-line BBC News article. (12 March 2014)(http://www.bbc.co.uk/news/uk-26540635) Accesses 9 April 2014.
10. Rheingold, H.: *Tools for Thought.* MIT Press. (1983)
11. Rucker, R.: *Mind Tools.*Penguin Books. (1987)
12. Landauer, T.K.: *The Trouble with Computers .* MIT Press. (1996)
13. Licklider, J.C.R.: *Man-Computer Symbiosis.* (1960)
14. Engelbart, E.: *Augmenting Human Intellect: A Conceptual Framework.* (1962)
15. Kurzweil, R.: *The Singularity is Near.* (2005)
16. Carroll, J.B.: *Language, Thought and Reality.* (1956)
17. Radley, A.: Computers as Self., Proceedings of the 4th International Conference in Human-Computer Interaction, Tourism and Cultural Heritage, (2013).
18. Radley, A.: Self as Computer - 2015.
19. Radley, A.: Humans versus Computers Systems and Machines; a Battle for Freedom, Equality and Democracy, keynote paper, Proceedings of the 6th International Conference in Human-Computer Interaction, Tourism and Cultural Heritage, (2015).
20. Shannon, Claude, E.: *A Mathematical Theory of Communication.* (1949)
21. Shannon, Claude, E.: Theory of Secret Systems.
22. Rivest, Ronald, A Method for Obtaining Digital Signatures and Public Key Encryption CryptoSystems.
23. MacKay, Donald, Information, Mechanism and Meaning, The MIT Press, 1969

WHY SECURITY IS ALL ABOUT COPIES

1. Wrixen, Fred, Codes and Cyphers. (2005)
2. Kelly, K.: *What Technology Wants.* (2011)

Hackers don't want to damage computers any more, they want to own them. They've started to run direct attacks where just one business, or even just one computer, is infected. - Eugene Kaspersky

Benches and books have things in common beyond the fact that they're generally to do with sitting. Both are forms of public privacy, intimate spaces widely shared. - Mal Peet

3. Poster, M: *The Mode of Information.* (1990)
4. Fuller, B.: *Synergetics, Explorations in the Geometry of Thinking.* New York. Macmillan. (1975)
5. Bauman, Z.: *Liquid Modernity.* (2000)
6. Kurzwell, R.: The *Singularity is Near.* (2005)

AETIOLOGY OF A SECURE NETWORK

1. Human Brain Project: European Commission Project. See: https://www.humanbrainproject.eu/en_GB. Accessed 10th April 2014.
2. DeRose, S., Bringsjord: *Are Computers Alive,* Abacus, Vol. 2, No. 4, (1985) Springer-Verlag, New York, Inc.
3. Turing, A.: *Computing Machinery and Intelligence.* Mind. (1950)
4. Ayer, A.: *Language, Truth and Logic.* (1936)
5. Wittgenstein, L.: *Logisch-Philosophische.* (1921)
6. Wittgenstein, L.: *Tractatus Logico-Philosophicus.* (1922)
7. Kelly, K.: *What Technology Wants.* (2011)
8. Arthur, W.B.: *The Nature of Technology.* (2009)
9. Watson, Richard.: *Future Minds: How the Digital Age is Changing Our Minds, Why this Matters and What We Can Do About It.,* (2010)
10. Talbott, Steve.: *The Future Does Not Compute: Transcending the Machines in our Midst.* (1995)
11. Lanier, Jaron.: *Who Owns the Future,* Penguin (2013)

BUILDING ACTOR-COHERENT DEFENCES

12. Plato.: *Collected Dialogues.*
13. Heisenberg, Werner.: *Physics and Philosophy.* (1962)
14. Penrose, Roger. *The Road to Reality: A Complete Guide to the Laws of the Universe.* (2007)
15. Tresch, John.: *The Romantic Machine: Utopian Science and Technology After Napoleon.* (2012)
16. Weizenbaum, J.: *Computer Power and Human Reason.* (1976)
17. Wertheimer, M.: *Productive Thinking.* (1959)

PRIMARY-NETWORK DESIGN

1. Baxi, Upendra.: *The Future of Human Rights.* (2012)
2. Veltman Kim.: *Understanding New Media.* (2006)
3. Nelson, Ted.: *Geeks Baring Gifts.,* (2013)
4. Veltman Kim.: *The Alphabet of Life,* (2014)
5. McLuhan, Marshall.: *Understanding Media: The Extensions of Man.,* (1964)
6. McLuhan, Marshall.: *The Global Village: Transformations in World Life and Media in the 21st Century.,* (1989)
7. Shannon, Claude, E.: *A Mathematical Theory of Communication.* (1949)
8. *Universal Declaration of Human Rights.* UN General Assembly. (1948)
9. Volokh, Eugene (2000).: "*Freedom of Speech, Information Privacy, and the Troubling Implications of a Right to Stop People from Speaking about You*". Stanford Law Review 52 (5): 1049–1124. doi:10.2307/1229510.

It is often said, but in the modern world it is a matter of *when*, rather than *if*, your organisation will be forced to deal with a cyber attack. 70 per cent of firms have suffered a "significant" breach in the last year, but that does not mean nothing is being done to fight the threat. "The threat is probably as big as it was five years ago, but that does not mean we have not had success," said one expert. "It could have been a whole lot worse if we were doing nothing." - Business Reporter 2015

Privacy under what circumstance? Privacy at home under what circumstances? You have more privacy if everyone's illiterate, but you wouldn't really call that privacy. That's ignorance. - Bruce Sterling

NOTES   89

10. Solove, Daniel J. (2003).: *The Virtues of Knowing Less: Justifying Privacy Protections against Disclosure.* Duke Law Journal 53 (3): 967–1065 [p. 976]. JSTOR 1373222.

11. Mayes, Tessa (18 March 2011): "We have no right to be forgotten online". The Guardian.

12. *Mumford,L.:The Myth of the Machine: Volume 1.*(1971)

ENCRYPTION THEORY

1. *Development:The Myth of the Machine: Volume 1.,*(1971)
2. Hofstadter, Douglas, R.: *Godel, Escher and Bach:An Eternal Golden Braid.*,(1979)
3. Hofstadter, Douglas, R.: *Surfaces and Essences.,* (2013)
4. Aristotelian Society. *Men and Machines; Symposia Read at the Joint Session of the Aristotelian Society and the Mind Association at Birmingham (July 11th-13th 1952.)* Harrison and Sons Ltd.
5. Berleant, Daniel.: *The Human Race to The Future:What could happen - and What to do.,*(2014)
6. Stiegler, Bernard.: *Technicity.,*(2013)
7. Bell, Wendell.: *Foundations of Futures Studies (Volumes 1 and 2).,*(2004,2010).
8. Lanier, Jaron.:*Who Owns the Future,* Penguin, (2013)
9. Mitchell, William, J.: *Me++; The Cyborg Self and the Networked City.,* (2003)
10. Baxi, Upendra.: *The Future of Human Rights.*,(2012)

THE BEHOLDER'S SHARE

1. Laurel, B.: *Computers as Theatre.,* Addison-Wesley Publishing Company Inc. (1991)
2. Sutherland, I.: *Sketchpad – A Man Machine Graphical Communication System.* AFIPS Conference meeting. (1963)
3. Johnson,J., et al.:*The Xerox "Star:A Retrospective".* Online Article: http://members.dcn.org/dwnelson/XeroxStarRetrospective.html. Retrieved 2013-08-13.
4. Hiltzik, M.A.: *Dealers of Lightening, Zerox PARC and the Dawn of the Computer Age.* Harper Collins, New York. (1999)
5. Gombrich, E.: *Art and Illusion.* Phaidon Press Ltd. (1960)
6. Brand, S.: *The Media Lab: Inventing The Future at M.I.T.,* p. 144. R.R.Donnelley and Sons., USA. (1989)
7. Veltman, K.H.: *Linear Perspective and the Visual Dimensions of Science and Art.* Deutscher Kunstverlag. (1986)

BIGGER-BRAIN VS STEALTH

1. Kennedy, Barbar, M., Bell, David.: *Cybercultures and the World we Live in. The Cybercultures Reader.,* (2000).
2. Rushkoff, Douglas.: *Cyberia: Life in the Trenches of Hyperspace.,*(1994).
3. Veltman Kim.: *The Alphabet of Life,* (2014).
4. Veltman Kim.: *Understanding New Media,* (2006).
5. Rose, N.: *Inventing Ourselves.*
6. Prince Philip.: HRH The Duke of Edinburgh. *Men, Machines and Sacred Cows.*,(1982).

There was of course no way of knowing whether you were being watched at any given moment. How often, or on what system, the Thought Police plugged in on any individual wire was guesswork. It was even conceivable that they watched everybody all the time. but at any rate they could plug in your wire whenever they wanted to. You have to live - did live, from habit that became instinct - in the assumption that every sound you made was overheard, and, except in darkness, every movement scrutinised. - George Orwell

NSA can't trust brilliant people, they intend to replace sysadmins with computer programs!

7. Berleant, Daniel.: *The Human Race to The Future: What could happen - and What to do.,* (2014).
8. Wells, Herbert, George.: *World Brain.,* (1936).
9. Gaines, Brian, R.: *Convergence to the Information Highway,* (1996).
10. Otlet, Pual. Monde: *Essai d'universalisme,* (1935).
11. Bush, Vannevar.: *As We May Think.* The Atlantic, (1945).
12. Licklider, J.C.R.: *Man-Computer Symbiosis.,* (1960).
13. Rheingold, Howard.: *Tools for Thought.* MIT Press, (1983).
14. Hafner, Katie., Lyon, Matthew.: *Where Wizards Stay Up Late: The Origins of the Internet.,* (1998).
15. Aspray, William.: *Computer: A History of the Information Machine.,* (2004).
16. Barrett, Neil.: *The Binary Revolution: The History and Development of the Computer.,* (2006).
17. Nelson, Ted.: *Geeks Baring Gifts.,* (2013).
18. Nelson, Ted.: *Possiplex - An Autobiography of Ted Nelson.,* (2011).
19. Buckland, Michael. Emanuel Goldberg and His Knowledge Machine. (2006).

PRIVACY AND SECURITY - THE BIG PICTURE

1. Nelson, Ted.: *Geeks Baring Gifts.,* (2013).
2. Nelson, Ted.: *Computer Lib / Dream Machines,* (1974).
3. Nelson, Ted.: *The Hypertext,* Proceedings of the World Documentation Federation, (1965).
4. Nelson, Ted.: *A File Structure for the Complex, The Changing and the Indeterminate. Complex Information Processing,* proceedings of the ACM 20th national conference 1965, (1965).
5. Nelson, Ted.: *Literary Machines,* (1982).
6. Radley, A.: Computers as Self., Proceedings of the 4th International Conference in Human-Computer Interaction, Tourism and Cultural Heritage, (2013).
7. Veltman, Kim.: *Frontiers in Conceptual Navigation for Cultural Heritage,* (2001).
8. Veltman, Kim.: *Towards a Semantic Web for Culture,* (2004).
9. Veltman, Kim.: *Understanding New Media.*
10. Wells, Herbert, George.: *World Brain.,* (1936).
11. Otlet, Pual.: Monde: *Essai d'universalisme,* (1935).
12. Bush, Vannevar. *As We May Think.* The Atlantic, (1945).
13. Buckland, Michael. Emanuel Goldberg and His Knowledge Machine. (2006).
14. Veltman Kim.: *The Alphabet of Life,* (2014).

A THEORY OF ABSOLUTE SECURITY

1. Woolley, Benjamin.: *Virtual Worlds.,* (1994).
2. Rheingold Howard.: *Virtual Reality.,* (1991).
3. Markley, Robert.: *Virtual Realities and Their Discontents.,* (1995).
4. Blascovich, Jim, Bailenson, Jeremy. *Infinite Reality: Avatars, Eternal Life, New Worlds, and the Dawn of the Virtual Revolution.,* (2011).
5. Artaud, Antonin.: *The Theatre and its Double.,* (1938).
6. Lanham, Richard.: *The Electronic Word.,* (1995).
7. Phillip Rogaway, The Moral Failure of Computer Scientists, The Atlantic, 2016.

DDOS Attack - A distributed **denial-of-service (DDoS) attack** occurs when multiple systems flood the bandwidth or resources of a targeted system, usually one or more web servers. Such an attack is often the result of multiple compromised systems (for example a botnet) flooding the targeted system with traffic.

Glossary - *includes coined terms*

- approx. 70 (ostensibly) new terms - not all are listed (standard ones capitalised)

Absolute Security [TARGET] - for a point-to-point communication system - is the replication of a single instance (or *primary-copy*) of a datum - from one socially restricted access-node to another. In other words, it is the **single-copy-send** of a datum from one party to another; whereby no - socially accessible - nth-party copies exist whatsoever (hopefully persistently).

Absolute Security [METHOD(S)] - are continually working security: systems, rules, actors, networks, programs, defences and human / automatic operational procedures etc; that protect: An Absolute Security <u>TARGET</u>.

Access - Ability of an actor (or human) to see, know and/or change an item.

ACCESS CONTROL - Restricting access to resources to privileged entities.

Access-Device - Physical access device that enables a human to gain entry into a primary/secondary/tertiary network (i.e. a personal computer).

Access-Node - Virtual access gateway (login-node / point-of-entry) for a primary/secondary/tertiary network.

ACCESS-MANAGEMENT - Protective methods for specific network access-node(s) - may involve management of User Identity, Secret Passwords etc - and the creation of protective techniques / access gateways for the system.

Access-Media - is a hardware / software system that enables an actor to see, *know* and/or *change* a copy's form and/or content.

Access-Gateway - consists of one or more access-nodes and/ or exposed attack-surface(s) - for a primary, secondary or tertiary copy. The gateway is comprised of a group of hardware / software elements that together form an 'entrance aperture' for actor pathway(s). The gateway may be - open or shut - protected or unprotected - at any particular place / time - and for specific actor(s) / attack- vector(s) - and by means of access / locking mechanism(s).

Actor-Coherence (Defence) - is when all of the actors, entities and processes - present in a primary-network's data- processing stack - are impelled to act together in order to protect the private datum-copy's form and/or content from unwarranted social access (hopefully for all places / times).

Actor-Integrity - Unity of (data-processing) action (for all actors on the data-processing stack).

> We are now aware of a terrifying reality—that governments don't necessarily need intermediaries like Facebook, Google, and Microsoft to get our data. They can intercept it over undersea cables, through secret court orders, and through intelligence sharing. - Privacy International

It's important to be informed about issues like usability, reliability, security, privacy, and some of the inherent limitations of computers. - Brian Kernighan

Actor Unity-of-Purpose - Unity of purpose and/or design (for all actors on the data-processing stack).

ALGORITHM - A series of instructions whereby a mathematical formula is applied to the numeric representation of a message in order to encrypt or decrypt it.

ATTACK-SURFACE - is an exposed facet / system entry-point for a datum-copy, existing on a primary-network's data-processing stack, and which (potentially) facilitates unwarranted social access to a private datum-copy's content and/or form.

ATTACK-VECTOR - is a specific data-processing path, existing on a primary-network's data-processing stack - which (potentially) provides unwarranted social access to a private datum-copy's content and/or form.

AUTHENTICATION - The process of verifying the sender or receiver as well as the contents of a communication. Conveyance, to another entity, of official sanction to do or be something.

Secondary-Copy - is a replication of a *primary-copy* - existing within (or outside) the boundaries of a point-to-point communication system - that may be legitimately produced by the communication process itself; and/or be illegitimately created as a result of the unwarranted activities of a hacker.

BACK-DOOR - is an access-gateway provided by a primary-network vendor - that (possibly) enables one or more actors to bypass network security system(s) and obtain unauthorised access to private datum(s).

BEHOLDER'S SHARE - Art historian Sir Earnest Gombrich (1909-2001) first defined the "***beholder's share***" - which states that our perceptual experience – depends on the active interpretation of sensory input. Perception becomes a generative act, one in which biological and sociocultural influences conspire to shape the brain's 'best guess' of the causes (and meaning) of its sensory signals - or in our terms the meaning of the symbolic message being communicated. In the context of security systems - the Beholder's Share refers to methods for protecting meaning gateway(s) by means of secret/private modal contexts / interpretation(s) for communicated datum(s).

BINARY - having two components or possible states, usually represented by ones and zeros in varies patterns.

BIT - the smallest unit of information in a computer. Equivalent to a single zero or one. The word bit is a contraction of binary-digit.

The institutions that we've built up over the years to protect our individual privacy rights from the government don't apply to the private sector. The Fourth Amendment doesn't apply to corporations. The Freedom of Information Act doesn't apply to Silicon Valley. And you can't impeach Google if it breaks its 'Don't be evil' campaign pledge. - Al Franken

Civilization is the progress toward a society of privacy. The savage's
whole existence is public, ruled by the laws of his tribe. Civilization is
the process of setting man free from men. - Ayn Rand   GLOSSARY   93

CENTRAL-SERVER (Network) - Refers to
cloud-server networks; such as email, Dropbox, Facebook,
Twitter etc; in which all of the communicated data is relayed by -
and stored on - centralised storage facilities.

CERTIFICATION - Endorsement of information by a trusted entity.

CASTLE-DEFENCE - See Depth-Defence definition.

CLOUD - See Central-Server definition.

CODE - (French, Latin: 'tree-trunk, 'writing tablet') - A method
of concealment that may use words, numbers or syllables to
replace original words / phrases of a message. Codes substitute
whole words whereas ciphers transpose or substitute letters or
digi-graphs. Also a disguised way of evoking meaning
(non-symbolic obfuscation).

CODEBOOK - Either a collection of code terms or a book
used to encode and decode messages.

CODE-NAMES - Name concealments for a person or object /
item / datum etc.

Code-numbers - Numbers that function like codewords
when they replace the words of a plaintext message.

CODE-TEXT - The result of encoding a given communication
(the plaintext). Similar to cipher-text, code-text differs mainly in
that a code, rather than a cipher, conceals the text.

Coding - is defined as the generation of descriptive and/or
selectional layers for a representation.

Copy - Shorthand for Datum-Copy.

Content (Datum-Copy) - refers to the meaning
content of a communicated datum. A representation (or
datum) may have metrical, descriptive and selectional aspects -
which work together to convey meaning.

COMMUNICATION (Human) - Transfer of discrete
package(s) of meaning - messages - between people; or the one-to-one
replication of datum(s) between minds + nominal meta-data (perhaps).

CRYPTOGRAPHY - is defined as a secret manner of writing,
either by arbitrary characters in other than the ordinary sense, or by
methods intelligible only to those possessing a (private) key.

CYBER - Relating to or characteristic of the culture of
computers, information technology, and virtual reality: the cyber age.

Sir Tim Berners-Lee said in 2013: 'a growing tide of surveillance and
censorship now threatens the future of democracy. Bold steps are
needed now to protect our fundamental rights to privacy and freedom
of opinion and association online.' [gizmodo.com-01.12.2013]

People are worried about privacy, and its one of the reasons people are using a service like SnapChat. - Peter Thiel

CYBER-ATTACK - An attempt by an unauthorised actor (person or computing agent) - to penetrate a digital system's security and gain unwarranted access to private / secret datum(s) contained therein.

CYBER-SECURITY - Defensive methods / mechanisms and/or security protocols (user ID's, passwords, secret keys etc) - that are employed to prevent any unwarranted actors from gaining unauthorised access to private / secret datum(s).

CYPHER - a secret or disguised way of writing (symbolic obfuscation). Also a method of concealment in which the primary unit is the letter.

CIPHER ALPHABET - An alphabet composed of substitutes for the normal alphabet or the particular alphabet in which the cipher is written.

CLEAR TEXT - A communication sent without encoding or encryption. Such messages are also called *in clear*, or sometimes *in plain language*.

CRYPTOGRAM - An encoded or enciphered message.

Cypher-Matching - Security protocol for defending a network communication instance - whereby (prior to sending any private information / datum(s)) the sender access-node asks the receiver access-node to decrypt and answer a specific (secret) question - and in order to establish the identity of the receiver with a reasonable degree of confidence.

CYPHER-TEXT - In cryptography, cypher-text is the result of encryption performed on plaintext using an algorithm, called a cipher. The new enciphered communication is the cipher-text.

DATA INTEGRITY - Ensuring information has not been altered by unauthorized or unknown means.

Data-Processing Stack - the sum total of all the actors, entities and processes etc; existing on - and/or potentially influencing - a primary-network's communication 'pipeline'.

Datum - any idea or thing is a ***pattern of meaning***, an abbreviated description, definition or set of 'facts' concerning the thing in question; typically prescribing an event, object, feeling, etc.; in token of, as a sign, symbol, or evidence of something.

DEFENCE-IN-DEPTH - an approach to comprehensive information security - whereby network privacy is protected by means of nested protective layers - and the same - which may include stealth defences for closing / blocking / camouflaging access-gateways, plus multiple layers of encryption / coding and layered symbolic, meaning and selectional gateways etc.

As with so many significant privacy violations of late by government agencies, from the NSA to the IRS, it's become clear that technology has far outpaced the law. Federal laws (USA) meant to protect our fourth Amendment right 'to secure in [our] persons, houses, papers and effects, against unreasonable search and seizure' do not adequately cover American's property on-line. - Kevin Yoder

I'm giving into my tendency to want to blur and blend the
lines between art and life, and privacy and sharing. - Lia Ices

GLOSSARY   95

Descriptive Content - refers to matching each symbol
in a representation to its specific meaning - and according to the
common descriptive language employed.

Descriptive Attack-Surface - Relates to Descriptive
Content - whereby notably the sender and receiver may be using
an obscure coding language whereby the symbol-to-meaning
relationship is protected (i.e. red means big etc).

Datum-Copy - is a particular instantiation of a datum's
pattern - that exists inside or (potentially) outside of a
point-to-point communication system. Creation of a
datum-copy involves instantiation of form in place and time
(i.e. illustration of content in the real and/or virtual worlds).
A ***datum-copy*** is a particular instantiation of a datum's
pattern - that exists inside or (potentially) outside of a
point-to- point communication system.

Datum Meaning - refers to the de-coded meaning
content present in a datum's content; or to the specific ideas /
concepts that are to be conveyed.

DIGI-GRAPH (Greek: di, 'twice' + graphic, 'to write') - An
encipherment in which the plain-text is written using letter pairs.

DISTRIBUTED TRANSPORT - refers to the process of
distributed transport for digital packets - whereby in terms of a
single point-to-point communication instance - data-packets are
routed along different network paths - and hence through
different servers (normally reflection servers).

ENTITY AUTHENTICATION / IDENTIFICATION -
Corroboration of the identity of an entity (e.g a person, a
computer terminal etc).

ENVIRONMENTAL SPYING - spying on the
primary-network through leaking emanations, including radio
or electrical signals and vibration(s) etc.

Form (Datum-Copy) - A copy has two primary aspects:
firstly **form** (the encapsulating media of storage, communication /
delivery, and access) and secondly - **content** (see definition).

FRONT-DOOR - is an open access-gateway that may be
accessed by legitimate users; or else 'hacked' / broken-into
by illegitimate users; ergo a front-door enables actors to
bypass network security system(s) and obtain access to
private datum(s).

GEOMETRIC PATTERNS - Configurations used to align,
transpose or substitute alphabet letters with other letters,
numerals or special forms such as those of symbol cryptography.

Under current statute, US government agencies such as the IRS, DHS,
SEC and many others are allowed to access emails and other private
communications older than 180 days. - Kevin Yoder

Privacy is tremendously important. I believe the American people, and all people, should be skeptical of government power, should ask hard questions: What is the authority? What is the oversight? That's the way it ought to be.- James Comey

ENCRYPTION (Symbolic) - *Symbolic Encryption* is

the process of encrypting symbolic messages - or obfuscating datums consisting of patterns of symbols. Whereby information is encoded in such a way that only authorised parties can read it - typically by replacing / jumbling symbols according to a mathematical procedure which obscures the original symbolic pattern. In an encryption scheme, the intended communication of information, referred to as plaintext (i.e "Alan is tall"), is encrypted using a special algorithm, generating cipher-text that can only be read if decrypted (i.e. "Bmbo jl umm").

HACKING - In the computer security context, a **hacker** is

someone who seeks and exploits weaknesses in a computer system or network. Hackers may be motivated by a multitude of reasons, such as profit, protest, challenge, enjoyment, or to evaluate those weaknesses to assist in removing them.

IDENTITY MANAGEMENT - describes the

management of individual identities (matching unique and specific human(s)) - and their authentication and authorisation - plus privileges within or across system and enterprise boundaries with the goal of increasing security and productivity while decreasing cost, downtime and repetitive tasks.

Illegitimate Secondary Copy - is a secondary-copy

that is/has-been created by an unwarranted party (or actor) - effectively a system hacker - the same being one who does not have permission to do the same, and/or to access the contained private datum(s).

INTERNET-PROTOCOL (IP) - is the principal

communications protocol in the Internet protocol suite for relaying datagrams across network boundaries. Each access device on the Internet is assigned a semi-unique (but possibly temporary) IP address for the purposes of identification during local and remote communication(s).

Invitation-Only Network - A special type of network

design in which members are required to invite each other onto respective private networks - whereby whilst the system may exist on an open network - communications on the invitation network cannot be made with non-members.

JARGON CODES - Open methods of linguistic concealment.

A type of open code, the jargon code is not hidden by symbols or transposed letters. Rather, an innocent word or words replaces another term in a sentence constructed in an innocuous fashion.

Private information protected by the little SIM card in your handset might not be so private after all. Based on new documentation from former NSA-employee turned-whistleblower, Edward Snowden, The Intercept is reporting on a state-sponsored theft of encryption keys from Gemalto; a company that makes 2 billion SIM cards annually.

I want to talk about privacy, the quality of the information you receive, whether it's neutral or commercial or pointed, bringing consciousness to the lack of neutrality in the algorithms. - Beeban Kidron

GLOSSARY   97

KeyMail - Multi-encrypted P2P electronic mail (developed by the author) that provides Absolute Security.

Legitimate Secondary Copy - is a secondary-copy that is/has-been created by a warranted party (or actor) - often the network system itself (e.g central-server copies) the same being one who has permission to do the same.

Local-Actor - A *local-actor* is a data processing unit - existing on a local access-device - comprised of either hardware and/or software elements — which (potentially) acts on a datum-copy's form and/or content within the primary-network's data-processing stack.

MAC ADDRESS - A unique identifier for a computer and/or other networked device (typically for use on an open-network such as the Internet).

MALWARE - is an umbrella term used to refer to a variety of forms of hostile or intrusive software, including computer viruses, worms, trojan horses, ransomware, spyware, adware, scareware, and other malicious programs. It can take the form of executable code, scripts, active content, and other software.

Meaning Gateway - an access-gateway that protects who (i.e. which human and/or automatic actor) can decode the meaning of a Datum-Copies inner datum(s). May consist of metrical (symbolic), descriptive, and selectional layers.

Memory Node - A computer node that acts as a storage medium for a Datum-Copy.

MESSAGE AUTHENTICATION - Corroborating the source of the information; also know as data origin authentication.

MESSAGE - The information pattern / datum-content to be transferred.

Metrical Content - For any representation, notably, the metrical aspect - or pattern of atomic facts / symbols - is always present - and works together with a descriptive aspect - to convey meaning.

Metrical Attack-Surface - Consists of a pattern of atomic facts/symbols used to convey meaning.

NSA - National Security Agency (USA).

Network-Actor - A *network-actor* is a data processing unit - existing on a remote networked-device - comprised of either hardware and/or software elements - which (potentially) acts on a datum-copy's form and/or content within the primary-network's data-processing stack.

With these stolen encryption keys, intelligence agencies can monitor mobile communications without seeking or receiving approval from telecom companies and foreign governments.

Privacy is a vast subject. Also, remember that privacy and convenience is always a trade-off. When you open a bank account and want to borrow some money, and you want to get a very cheap loan, you'll share all details of your assets because you want them to give you a low interest rate.- Nandan Nilekani

NULL - A meaningless letter, symbol or number inserted into a code list or cypher alphabet. Nulls are used to complicate decryption efforts of unintended 3rd-parties; by disrupting sentence patterns, word lengths and the frequency of syllable groups.

ONE-TIME-PAD - In cryptography the **one-time pad** (**OTP**) is an encryption technique that cannot be cracked if used correctly. In this technique, a plaintext is paired with a random secret key (also referred to as *a one-time pad*). Then, each bit or character of the plaintext is encrypted by combining it with the corresponding bit or character from the pad using modular addition. If the key is truly random, is at least as long as the plaintext, is never reused in whole or in part, and is kept completely secret, then the resulting cipher-text will be impossible to decrypt or break. However, practical problems have (often) prevented one-time pads from being widely used. The "pad" part of the name comes from early implementations where the key material was distributed as a pad of paper, so that the top sheet could be easily torn off and destroyed after use.

OPEN CODE - A code concealed in an apparently innocent message. Open codes are a branch of linguistically masked communications which includes null cyphers, geometric methods and jargon codes.

Open-Datum - is one that anyone may access - but *open-thoughts* are not a subject of this book (see Self-as-Computer).

Open-Network - refers to a network (such as the Internet) in which any number of access-nodes/devices may be connected and/or inter-communicate with few top-level rules - but only lower-level protocols. Traffic flows across an open network without any restrictions / controls.

PATTERN OBFUSCATION - refers to special encryption / coding / scrambling methods - employed to prevent spies from deducing information from patterns present in the copy.

PEER-TO-PEER or P2P NETWORK - such as Napster, BitCoin, BitTorrent etc; the same forming a distributed network of peer-to-peer nodes that render the communicated information directly available to network participants - without the need for centralised co-ordination. A key advantage of P2P is that 'participating users establish a virtual network, entirely independent from the physical network, without having to obey any administrative authorities or restrictions.'

Cryptography and Human Freedom

Cryptography should (most definitely) not be made illegal, as UK Prime Minister David Cameron recently suggested in February 2015. Cryptography is a natural requirement of the need to protect our secret and private thoughts. Our minds (and natural thoughts) are the natural property of individuals and collectives, and not ownerless material 'objects' that may be stolen, controlled and/or 'used' by others against our will.

Ideally, really ideally, you want to get to a place where you can have creative control over the material you create - choices, at least, anyway. And you want your choice of script and role. But do you really want your life to revolve around trying to maintain your privacy?- Jai Courtney

GLOSSARY 99

Partial Security - defined as a network which may possibly produce - or cause to come into existence - any unprotected - or nth-party accessible - *primary / secondary / tertiary datum-copies.*

PERFECT SECURITY - is the notion that, given an encrypted message (or cipher-text) from a **perfectly secure** encryption system (or cipher), absolutely nothing will be revealed about the unencrypted message (or plaintext) by the cipher-text.

PERFECT FORWARD SECURITY - is a feature of specific key agreement protocols that gives assurances your session keys will not be compromised even if the private key of the server is compromised.

Physical Gateway - refers to access-gateways related to the copy's physical representation - for example any gateways existing on media of storage, access and/or transport.

Physical Representation (Datum-Copy) - refers to an electronic / magnetic / optical 'container' for a datum-copy.

Primary-Copy - is a place-holder for a private datum of meaning - existing within the boundaries of a point-to-point communication system; whose content and form are restricted in terms of **social access** (i.e who can see, know & change the same); whereby the datum is (ideally) communicated via **single-copy-send** from the source point to any (and all) designated receiver point(s).

Primary-Network - is a provided point-to-point communication system; whereby a private **access-node** (the source point) exists on a networked **access-device**; which stores a primary-copy of a private-datum; prior to the single-copy-send of the same to a socially restricted access-node (the destination-point). A primary-network may create legitimate secondary-copies of the primary-copy.

PRIVACY - is defined as social restriction of an item (ie. an idea / thought / datum-copy etc) to two or more parties alone - whereby access to any related copies are protected / restricted for any and all other unwarranted persons / actors.

Private Communication - can be defined as protection of *privacy of meaning*; or the safe transfer of single / multiple datum(s) between humans.

Private-Datum - A *private-thought/datum* is distributed / available to a limited number of people; and hence some form of social sharing plus protection is implied; and in order to prevent it from morphing into an open-thought/datum.

Cryptography and Human Freedom

Cryptography is how thoughts defend themselves from attack, and it is how we can obtain freedom of mind, heart and body; and therefore cryptography is a part of our very humanity; and it must be recognized as a fundamental human right.

Anyone who steps back for a minute and observes our modern digital world might conclude that we have destroyed our privacy in exchange for convenience and false security. - John Twelve Hawks

Private-Thoughts - Thoughts which are shared amongst a restricted group of people.

Private-by-Guarantee - Maintenance of privacy for an item for an extended period of time - whereby there is no possibility of the item morphing into an open one - in terms of social access.

PUBLIC KEY ENCRYPTION - the (public) encryption key is published for anyone to use and encrypt messages. However, only the receiving party has access to the (private) decryption key that allows messages to be read.

Reflection Server - A server (existing on a communication network) which merely 'reflect's or directs packets from one location to another - and does not store any of these packets on the same server for extended periods of time.

SCRAMBLING (Data) - Jumbling and /or changing the order of a datum(s) symbols according to an (ostensibly) unreadable scheme and/or algorithm.

SCRAMBLING (Channel) - Jumbling and /or changing the order of a communication's data packets according to an (ostensibly) unreadable scheme and/or algorithm.

Secondary-Copy - is a replication of a *primary-copy* - existing within (or outside) the boundaries of a point-to-point communication system - that may be legitimately produced by the communication process itself; and/or be illegitimately created as a result of the unwarranted activities of a hacker.

Secondary-Network - is a privileged-access network intimately connected to the primary-network's communication pipeline; whereby copies of communicated private-datum(s) may exist on an nth-party organisational network and/or various local and/or central replication (backup) network(s). A secondary-network may contain legitimate replicated secondary-copies of primary-copies and/or other secondary-copies

SECRET-KEY - In cryptography, a private or secret key is an encryption/decryption key known only to the party or parties that exchange secret messages. In traditional secret key cryptography, a key would be shared by the communicators so that each could encrypt and decrypt messages.

SECRET-KEY MANAGEMENT - Protective methods for a specific secret-key - in order to protect the key from unwarranted social access.

Secret-Datum - (analogous to a *secret- thought*) - which has not yet left the source point (or sender's mind); and which is assumed to be unique in that nobody else can know (or discover) the precise **form** or **content** of the datum at the source point.

In Egyptian theology, the most singular organ of the Sun God Re, was the eye: for the Eye of Re had an independent existence and played a creative and directive part in all cosmic and human activities—the computer turns out to be the Eye of the re-instantiated Sun God, that is, The Eye of the Megamachine (masses of humans organised into companies for specific purposes), serving the 'Private Eye' or Detective, as well the omnipresent Executive Eye, he who exacts absolute conformity to his comrades, because no secret can be hidden from him, and no disobedience goes unpunished! - Lewis Mumford

Relying on the government to protect your
privacy is like asking a peeping tom to install your
window blinds. - John Perry Barlow   GLOSSARY   101

SECURITY - Accordingly, security - for a person-to-person communication system - can be defined as protection of *secrecy, privacy* or *openness of meaning*; or the safe transfer of single / multiple datum(s) between humans.

Selectional Content - refers to modal context(s) with respect to a representation - or modal constructive aspect(s) of the same.

Selectional Attack Surface - refers to a protective layer for any selectional (modal) context(s) present - and hence to the (potential) opening-up of any constructive aspect(s) for the representation.

Self-Computer - Merging of human(s) with computers/machines/systems/technology.

SEMAGRAM - A form of steganography, wherein encryptions are made of arrangements of objects, images, or symbols rather than by letters or numbers.

SHANNON'S MAXIM - (i.e. Kerckhoff's principle); assume that: **'the enemy knows the system'**. Avoid relying on **security through obscurity** and/or **security through minority** - in terms of assuming that the secrecy / uncommonness of system design provides unimpeachable protection.

SIGNATURE - A means to bind information to an entity.

Social Access - refers to humans gaining access to a datum-copies form and or content.

Stealth Network - refers to any network that employs stealth techniques and/or defensive mechanisms - to protect against / repeal - any unwarranted hackers/attacks; and in terms of excluding / disguising / blocking entry-point(s) for the primary-network's data-processing stack.

Single-Copy-Send - communication of a datum (+ meta-data) with guaranteed social security.

Socially Secure Communication - communication that protects socially restricted access (secrecy or privacy) for the replicated meaning - datum(s) + nominal meta-data (perhaps).

SPYING - refers to secret / unwarranted access to private items / ideas / datum(s) / concepts etc.

STEGANOGRAPHY - (Greek: steganos, 'covered' + graphein, 'writing') - A primary form of communications security that conceals the physical presence of a secret message, which may or may not be additionally protected by a code or cipher.

The revelations, which include backdoors built into some technologies, raise troubling questions about the security that hundreds of millions of people rely on to keep their most intimate and business-sensitive secrets private in an increasingly networked world.

Where and how to store data tops the list of priorities (for effective information security). Who to trust has also become a pertinent question when it comes to access management and procurement processes.

Privacy is not an option, and it shouldn't be the price we accept for just getting on the Internet. - Gary Kovacs

Storage Media - is a bundle of hardware / software technologies that work together to form a memory system - and in order to persist a datum-copy's form and content.

SYMMETRIC KEY ENCRYPTION - the encryption and decryption keys are the same. Communicating parties must have the same key before they can achieve secure communication.

Tertiary-Copy - is a replication of a *primary or secondary copy* - which is generated post-communication by extracting datum(s) from a large body of communication data (e.g. a transatlantic data pipe).

Tertiary-Network - is not directly connected to the primary- network - but nevertheless may still (belatedly) access data traffic flowing across primary and/or secondary-networks - resulting in illegitimate *tertiary-copies* of primary/secondary-copies.

Transfer Media - is a bundle of hardware / software technologies that work together to form a delivery system - and in order to send a datum-copy from a source-point to a destination-point.

TRANSMISSIONS SECURITY - An electronic form of communication security similar to steganography. Transmission security tries to hide the existence of secret messages in electrical exchanges, whether or not they are encrypted.

TROJAN HORSE - unsafe-actors misrepresenting as safe-actors.

UNBREAKABLE CIPHERS - include one-time methods and unconditionally secure crypto-systems.

Unsafe-Actor - An actor on the data-processing stack that is invisible / unknown / questionable in terms of purpose and/or integrity - and hence may (potentially) have undermined effects and/or progress unknown programming path(s).

USER-IDENTITY (ID) - individual identity for an actor on a network (perhaps matching unique / specific human(s))

VALIDATION - A means to provide timeliness of authorisation to use or manipulate information or resources.

Virtual Representation (Datum-Copy) - refers to an electronic / magnetic / optical 'container' for a datum-copy.

Virtual Gateway - refers to blocking mechanisms / hurdles with respect to the opening-up of a virtual representation of a datum copy.

VIRUS (computer) - is a malware program that, when executed, replicates by inserting copies of itself (possibly modified) into other programs, data files etc , and when this replication succeeds, the affected areas are then said to be 'infected'. A virus may or may not have harmful effects - and result in loss of privacy for private datum(s) etc.

The National Security Agency (NSA) and its British counterpart have successfully defeated encryption technologies used by a broad swath of online services, including those provided by Google, Facebook, Microsoft, and Yahoo; according to new reports published by *The New York Times*, *Pro Publica*, and *The Guardian*.

Bibliography

Abbott Abott, Edwin.: *Flatland.*(1884).

Anderson, Chris. *Free:The Future of a Radical Price.* New York, (2006).

Anderson, Walter, Truett.: *The Future of the Self.*,(1997).

Aristotelian Society.: *Men and Machines; Symposia Read at the Joint Session of the Aristotelian Society and the Mind Association at Birmingham (July 11th-13th 1952).* Harrison and Sons Ltd.

Aristotle., Barnes, Jonathan.: *The Complete Works of Aristotle; Volumes 1 and 2.*,(1984).

Armand, Louis., Bradley, Arthur., Zizek, Slavoj., Stiegler, Bernard.: *Technicity.*,(2013).

Arnasaon, H., H., Mansfield, Elizabeth, C.: *A History of Modern Art, 7th Edition.*, (2012).

Arthur, W.B.: *The Nature of Technology.*, (2009).

Ash, Brian.: *The Visual Encyclopaedia of Science Fiction.*, (1978).

Ashby, W.R.: *Introduction to Cybernetics.*,(1956).

Aspray, William.: *Computer: A History of the Information Machine.*, (2004).

Astounding Science Fiction Magazine: 1930s - 1980s

Asimov, I.: *I Robot.* (1940-1950)

Asimov, Isaac.: *Machines that Think: The Best Science Fiction Stories About Robots and Computers.*, (1985).

Asimov, Isaac.: *Robot Visions.*, (1991).

Auletta, Ken.: *Googled, The End of the World as We Know It.*, (2011).

Ayer, A.: *Language, Truth and Logic.* (1936)

Banks, Michael, A.: *On the Way to the Web: The Secret History of the Internet and its Founders.*,(2011).

Barrett, Neil.: *The Binary Revolution: The History and Development of the Computer.*,(2006).

Battelle, John.: *Search,* (2006).

Baxi, Upendra.: *The Future of Human Rights.*,(2012).

Baudrillard, J.: *Fatal Strategies.* ,(1983).

Baudrillard, Jean.: *Simulacra and Simulation.*,(1981).

Baudrillard, Jean.: *Simulations.*, (1983).

Bauman, Z.: Liquid Modernity. ,(2000).

Bell, Wendell.: *Foundations of Futures Studies (Volumes 1 and 2).*,(2004),(2010).

Berleant, Daniel.: *The Human Race to The Future: What could happen - and What to do.*,(2014).

Berners-Lee, Tim.: *Weaving the Web,* (1999).

Berry, Adrian.: *The Next Ten Thousand Years.*,(1975).

Blascovich, Jim, Bailenson, Jeremy.: *Infinite Reality: Avatars, Eternal Life, New Worlds, and the Dawn of the Virtual Revolution.*,(2011).

Bragdon, Claude, Fayette.: *A Primer of Higher Space (The Fourth Dimension).*,(1923).

Bradbury, Ray.: *Fahrenheit 451.*,(1953).

Brand, Stewart.: *The Clock of the Long Now: Time and Responsibility: The Ideas Behind the World's Slowest Computer.*,(2000).

Brand, S.: *The Media Lab: Inventing The Future at M.I.T.,* p. 144. R.R.Donnelley and Sons., USA.,(1989).

Brate, Adam.: *Technomanifestos: Visions of the Information Revolutionaries.*,(2002).

Brown, Jonathon.: *The Self.*,(2007).

Brunn, Stanely.: *Collapsing Space and Time.*,(1991).

Bolt, Richjard.: *The Human Interface, Where People and Computer Meet.*, (1984).

Boole, George.: *An Investigation into The Laws of Thought.*,(1854).

Bowman, D.A.: *3D User Interfaces, Theory and Practice.* Addision Wesley. ,(2004).

Buckland, Michael. Emanuel Goldberg and His Knowledge Machine. (2006). Burdea, George. C., Coiffet, Philippe.: *Virtual Reality Technology.,*(2003).

Bush, Vannevar.: *As We May Think.* The Atlantic, (1945).

Calabrese, Andrew et al.: *Communication, Citizenship and Social Policy.,*(1999).

Cassirer Ernst.: *The Myth of the State.,*(1961).

Cassirer Ernst.: *The Philosophy of Symbolic Forms: Volumes 1-3.,*(1965).

Cassirer, Ernst.: *The Problem of Knowledge: Philosophy, Science and History Since Hegel.* (1969).

Claeys, Gregory., Sargent, Lyman, Tower.: *The Utopia Reader.,*(1999).

Clarke, Arthur, C.: *The Exploration of Space.,*(2010).

Cohen, John.: *Human Robots in Myth and Science.,*(1966).

Cork, Richard.: *Vorticism and Abstract Art in the Machine Age (2 volumes).,*(1976).

Copleston, Frederick.: *A History of Philosophy; volumes 1-11.,* (1946-1974).

Cotton, Bob; Oliver, Richard.: *Understanding Hypermedia.* ,(1983).

Coxeter, H.S.M.: *Introduction to Geometry.,*(1989).

Daily Telegraph.: *Do we want to give them A License to Kill?* (November 15th 2013).

Dale, Rodney.: *Edwardian Inventions.,*(1979).

Dasgupta, S.: *A History of Indian Philosophy.* Volume 1.,(1940).

Dawkins, Richard.: *The Blind Watchmaker.* (1986).

de Bono, Edward.: *Lateral Thinking: An Introduction.,*(1999).

de Bono, Edward.: *The Mechanism of Mind.,*(1976).

de Bono, Edward.: *Eureka.,*(1979).

de La Mettrie, Julien, Offray.: *Man a Machine.,* (1748).

de Sola Pool, Ithiel.: *Technologies of Freedom.,*(1984).

de Vries, Leonard.: *Victorian Inventions.,* (1991).

Debord, Guy.: *Society of the Spectacle.,*(1984)

DeRose, S., Bringsjord: Are Computers Alive? Abacus, Vol. 2, No. 4, (1985). Springer-Verlag, New York, Inc.

Descartes, R.: *Mediations on First Philosophy.,*(1641).

Descartes, R.: *Discourse on the Method of Rightly Conducting the Reason, and Seeking Truth in the Sciences.,*(1637).

Deutsch, David.: *The Fabric of Reality: The Science of Parallel Universes - and Its Implications.,*(1998).

D.H.L Hieronimus, Meyerhoff, Zohara, J.: *The Future of Human Experience: Visionary Thinkers on the Science of Consciousness.,* (2013).

Dick, Philip, K.: *Eye in the Sky.,*(1957).

Dick, Philip, K.: *A Scanner Darkly.,*(1977).

Dick, Philip, K.: *Do Androids Dream of Electric Sheep.,*|(1968).

Dick, Philip, K.: *The Man in the High Castle.,*(1962).

Dick, Philip, K.: *The Minority Report.,*(1956).

Diderot, D.: *Pensees Philosopiques.* (1746)

Domhoff., G.W.: *Wealth, Income and Power.* On-line article: http://www2.ucsc.edu/whorulesame rica/power/wealth.html (accessed 7th April 2014).

Earnshaw, R.,A., Gigante, M.,A., Jones, H.: *Virtual Reality Systems.,* (1995).

Elliott, Anthony.: *Concepts of the Self.,*(2007).

Encyclopaedia Britannica: 11th Edition, 29th editions.

Logical/ethical thoughts can save man from himself; and computers are how.

Ram: 'Do you believe in the Users?' Crom: 'Sure I do!'

'If I didn't have a User, then who wrote me?' - Tron [1982]

Ernst, b.: *The Magic Mirror of M.C.Escher.* Taschen GmbH.,(2007).

Engelbart, E.: *Augmenting Human Intellect: A Conceptual Framework.*,(1962).

Flocon, A., Barre, A.: *Curvilinear Perspective,From Visual Space to the Constructed Image.* University of California Press.,(1992).

Fraser, J.,Y.: *The Voices of Time.*, (1981).

Frewin, Anthony.: *One Hundred Years of Science Fiction Illustration.*,(1988).

Frauenfelder, Mark. *The Computer: An Illustrated History.*, (2013)

Freud, S.: *The Interpretation of Dreams.* (1899)

Forster, E.M.: *The Machine Stops.*,(1909).

Foucault, Michel.: *Discipline and Punishment: The Birth of the Prison.* Penguin,(1975).

Foucault, Michel.: *The Order of Things: An Archaeology of the Human Sciences.*,(1966).

Fuller, R. Buckminster.: *Operating Manual for Spaceship Earth.*, (1969).

Fuller, Buckminster.: *Synergetics, Explorations in the Geometry of Thinking.* New York. Macmillan.,(1975).

Fuller, R. Buckminster.: *Utopia or Oblivion: The Prospects for Humanity.*,(1972).

Gelernter, David.: *Mirror Worlds: or the Day Software Puts the Universe in a ShoeBox... How it will Happen and What it Will Mean.*,(1993).

George, Frank.: *Man the Machine.*,(1979).

Gibson, J.J.: *Th Ecological Approach to Visual Perception.* Psychology Press.,(1986).

Gibson,William.: *Neuromancer*, (1984).

Ginsberg, Morris.: *On the Diversity of Morals.*,(1957).

Gleick, James.: *The Information: A History, A Theory, A Flood.*, (2012).

Gabor, D.: *Innovations: Scientific, Technological, and Social.*, (1970).

Gombrich, E.: *Art and Illusion.* Phaidon Press Ltd. (1960)

Gray, Chris, Hables.: *Cyborg Citizen; Politics in the Posthuman Age.*,(2002).

Grau, Oliver.: *Virtual Art.*, (2004).

Grills, Chad.: *Future Proof: Mindsets for 21st Century Success.*, (2014).

Hafner, Katie., Lyon, Matthew.: *Where Wizards Stay Up Late: The Origins of the Internet.*,(1998).

Halacy, D.S.: *Cyborg: Evolution of the Superman.*,(1965).

Hamelink, Cees, J.: *The Ethics of Cyberspace.*,(2000).

Hamit, Francis.: *Virtual Reality and the Exploration of Cyberspace.*, (1993).

Haraway, Donna.J., Hables-Gray, Chris., Eglash, Ron., Clynes, Manfred.E.: *The Cyborg Handbook.*, (1995).

Henderson, Linda, Dalrymple.: *The Fourth Dimension and Non-Euclidean Geometry in Modern Art.*,(1983).

Heppenheimer T.A.: *Colonies in Space.*,(1977).

Heil, John.: *The Nature of True Minds.*,(1992).

Heidegger, Martin.: *Being and Time.*,(1927).

Heidegger, Martin.: *What is Called Thinking?*,(1976).

Heim, Michael. *The Metaphysics of Virtual Reality.*,(1994).

Hertzfeld,Andy.: *Revolution in the Valley.*, (2011).

Hiltzik, M.A.: *Dealers of Lightening, Zerox PARC and the Dawn of the Computer Age.* Harper Collins, New York.,(1999).

Understand and represent the true nature of thought; its integrated nature.

We need one simple system for everything!

To have a clean data structure from which you can do allot more. - Ted Nelson

Human beings are not meant to lose their
anonymity and privacy. - Sarah Chalke

Hinton, Charles, Howard.: *The Fourth Dimension.*,(1913).

Hobbes, Thomas.: *Leviathan.*,(1668).

Hodges, Andrew., Hofstadter, Douglas.: *Alan Turing: The Enigma.*,(1982).

Hofstadter, Douglas, R.: *Godel, Escher and Bach: An Eternal Golden Braid.*,(1979).

Hofstadter, Douglas, R.: *Surfaces and Essences.*, (2013).

Hofstadter, Douglas, R.: *The Mind's I: Fantasies and Reflections on Self and Soul.*, (1982).

Hofstadter Douglas.: *Metamagical Themas: Questing for the Essence of Mind and Pattern.*, (1986).

Holtzman, Steve, R.: *Digital Mantras: The Language of Abstract and Virtual Worlds.*, (1995).

Howard, I.P, Rogers, B.J.: *Binocular Vision and Stereopsis.* Oxford University Press. (1995)

Howe, Jeff.: *Crowdsourcing: Why the Power of the Crowd is Driving the Future of Business.*, (2009)

Human Brain Project: European Commission Project. See: https://www.humanbrainproject.eu/en_GB. Accessed (10th April 2014).

Hume, David.: *A Treatise on Human Nature.*, (1738).

Hume, Robert, Ernest.: *The Thirteen Principal Upanishads.*, (2010).

Hunger Statistics, United Nations World Food Programme.,(2013).

Husserl, Edmund. *Ideas: A General Introduction to Phenomenology: Volumes 1-3.*,(1913-).

Husserl, Edmund, Gustav, Albrecht.: *Logical Investigations.*, (1900).

Huxley, Aldous.: *Brave New World.*,(1931).

Jacobson, Linda.: *CyberArts: Exploring Art and Technology.*,(1992).

Johnson, George.: *In the Palaces of Memory: How We Build the Worlds Inside Our Heads.*,(1992).

Johnson, J., et al.: *The Xerox "Star: A Retrospective.* Online Article: http://members.dcn.org/dwnelson/XeroxStarRetrospective.html. Retrieved 2013-08-13.

Jarvis, Jeff.: *What Would Google Do?,* (2001).

Jung, C.: *Archetypes and the Collective Unconscious.*,(1959).

Jung, Carl.: *Man and His Symbols,* (1968).

Jung, C.G.,: Hull, R.F.C. *The Collected Works of Carl Jung (Volumes 1-20).*,(1960-1990).

Kant, Immanuel.: *Critique of Pure Reason.*,(1787).

Kahn, David.: *The Code Breakers: The Comprehensive History of Secret Communication from Ancient Times to the Internet.*, (1996).

Kelly, K.: *What Technology Wants.*,(2011).

Kent, Ernest, W.: *The Brains of Men and Machines.*,(1980).

Kery, Patricia, Frantz.: *Art Deco Graphics.*,(1986).

Kirk, G.S., Raven, J.E.: *The Pre-Socratic Philosophers.*,(1969).

Kirkpatrick, David.: *The Facebook Effect: The Inside Story of the Company That is Connecting the World.*,(2011).

Klee, Paul.: *Notebooks of Paul Klee (Volumes 1 and 2),* (1964, 1992).

Koepsell, David, R.: *The Ontology of Cyberspace: Philosophy, Law and the Future of Intellectual Property.*, (2003).

Krueger, Myron.: *Artificial Reality 2.* (1991).

Kurzweil, Ray.: *The Age of Spiritual Machines: When Computers Exceed Human Intelligence.*,(1999).

True nature of thought. Hyper-thought(s) in hyper-context(s).
Parallel linkages, overlays, comments etc. True nature of thinking.
Hyper-reality. Multiple thought-space(s), all connected.

Laithwaite, Eric.: *An Inventor in the Garden of Eden.*,(1994).

Lanier, Jaron.: *Who Owns the Future,* Penguin, (2013).

Lanier, Jaron.: *You are Not a Gadget: A Manifesto.*, (2001).

Landauer, Thomas, K.: *The Trouble with Computers: Usefulness, Usability, and Productivity.*,(1996).

Laurel, Brenda.: *The Art of the Human Computer Interface.*, (1990).

Laurel, B.: *Computers as Theatre.* Addison-Wesley Publishing Company Inc. ,(1991).

Leibniz, Gottfried Wilhelm.: *Philosophical Papers and Letters: Volumes 1 and 2.*, 1976, (2011).

Lemert, C.: *Thinking the Unthinkable, The Riddles of Classical Social Theories.*,(2007).

Lem, Stanislaw.: *The Cyberiad: Fables for the Cybernetic Ward.*, (1976).

Levy, Steven.: *How the NSA nearly destroyed the Internet.* Wired Magazine, January (2014).

Levy, Stephen.: *In the Plex; How Google Things, Works, and Shapes Our Lives.*, (2012).

Lewis, Arthur, O.: *Of Men and Machines.*,(1963).

Licklider, J.C.R.: *Man-Computer Symbiosis.*,(1960).

Lilley, S.: *Men, Machines and History.*, (1948).

Linzmayer, Owen. *Apple Confidential 2.0*, 2004.

Locke, John.: *An Essay Concerning Human Understanding.*,(1689).

Lombardo, Thomas.: *Contemporary Futurist Thought: Science Fiction, Future Studies, and Theories and Visions of the Future in the Last Century.*,(2006).

Lovejoy, Arthur, O.: *The Great Chain of Being: A Study of the History of an Idea.*,(1936).

Lovelock, James.: *Gaia.*

Lovelock, James.: *A Rough Ride to the Future,*(2014).

Luppicini, Rocci.: *Handbook of Research on Technoself: Identity in a Technological Society.*, (2012).

MacKay, Donald, Information, Mechanism and Meaning, The MIT Press, 1969

Mannheim, Karl.: *Ideology and Utopia: An Introduction to the Sociology of Knowledge.*,(1955).

Markley, Robert.: *Virtual Realities and Their Discontents.*,(1995|).

Markoff, John.: *From Counterculture to Cyberculture: Stewart Brand, the Whole Earth Network and the Rise of Digital Utopianism.*, (2008).

Markoff, John.: *What the Dormouse Said: How the Sixties Counterculture Shaped the Personal Computer Industry.*,(2006).

Marx, Carl., Engels, Friedrich.: *The Communist Manifesto.*,(1848).

Marx, K.: *Das Kapital.*,(1867).

Maslow, A.: *Motivation and Personality.*,(1954).

Merleau-Ponty, Maurice.: *Signs.*, (1964).

Merleau-Ponty, Maurice.: *Nature.*,(2000).

Menezes, ALfred, J., von Oorschot, Paul, C., Vanstobe, Scott, A.: *Handbook of Applied Cryptography.*,(1996).

McLuhan, Marshall.: *The Mechanical Bride: Folklore of Industrial Man.*, (1967).

McLuhan, Marshall.: *Understanding Media: The Extensions of Man.*,(1964).

McLuhan, Marshall.: *The Global Village: Transformations in World Life and Media in the 21st Century.*, (1989).

Mill, John, Stuart.: *On Liberty.*, (1859).

Mitchell, William. J.: *e-topia.*,(2000).

Mitchell, William, J.: *Me++; The Cyborg Self and the Networked City.*, (2003).

Moore, G., E.: *Principia Ethica.*,(1966).

Many ostensibly defensive techniques for privacy / security - may also be used as weaponised tools for the purposes of attack/hacking. For example, an attacker may use encryption or data/ID anonymity to hide his/her identity; or else hide their own MAC/IP address - plus the destination address for stolen data; alternatively an attacker may use distributed / flooding methods (DDoS attack) as part of an infiltration / attack strategy.

More, Max., Vita-More, Natasha.: *The Transhumanist Reader: Classical and Contemporary Essays on the Science, Technology and Philosophy of the Human Future.,*(2013).
More, Thomas.: *Utopia.,* (1516).
Moritz, Michael.: *Return to the Little Kingdom: Steve Jobs and the Creation of Apple.,* (2010).
Morrison, E.: *Men, Machines and Modern Times.,*(1966).
Mudrick, Marvin.: *The Man in the Machine.,* (1977).
Muller, Max.: *Sacred Books of the East: The Texts of Taoism.,* (1891).
Mumford, Lewis.: *The Pentagon of Power: The Myth of the Machine.,*(1970).
Mumford, Lewis.: *Technics and Human Development: The Myth of the Machine: Volume 1.,*(1971).
Murrell, Hywel.: *Men and Machines.,*(1976).

Nagel, Ernest.: *The Structure of Science.,*(1961).
Nelson, Ted.: *Computer Lib / Dream Machines,*(1974).
Nelson, Ted.: *Geeks Baring Gifts.,* (2013).
Nelson, Ted.: *Possiplex - An Autobiography of Ted Nelson.,* (2011).
Nietzsche, F.: *The Wanderer and his Shadow.,*(1880).
Nietzsche, F.: *Daybreak.,*(1880).
Nietzsche, F.: *Thus spoke Zarathustra.,*(1883).
Norman, Donald, A.: *The Invisible Computer.,* (1999).

O'Brien, Fitz, James.: *The Diamond Lens.,*(1858).
O-Neill, Gerard, K.: *2081: A Hopeful View of the Human Future.,* (1981).
Omni Magazine: Complete Collection
Orwell, George.: *Animal Farm.,* (1949).

Orwell, George.: *Nineteen Eight-Four.* Secker and Warburg, London, (1949).
Otlet, Pual.: Monde: *Essai d'universalisme,* (1935).
Ouspensky, P.D.: *A New Model of the Universe.,*(1969).
Ouspensky, P.D.: *In Search of the Miraculous.,* (1949).

Panofsky, E.: *Perspective as a symbolic form.* Zone Books. (1997)
Penrose, Roger.: *The Road to Reality: A Complete Guide to the Laws of the Universe.,*(2007).
Pinker, Steven.: *How the Mind Works.,*(2009).
Pinker, Steven.: *The Stuff of Thought: Language as a Window into Human Nature.,* (2008).
Plato.: Collected Dialogues.
Plato.: Cornford, Franics., M. *Plato's Theory of Knowledge: The Theaetetus and The Sophist Plato.,*(1957).
Ploman, Edward, W., Hamilton, L. Clark.: *Copyright: Intellectual Property in the Information Age.,*(1980).
Popper, Karl, J.: *The Open Society and It's Enemies (Volume 1 and 2).,*(1971).
Portola Institute.: *The Whole Earth Catalogue.,* (1972) Edition, (1986) Edition, (1995) Edition.
Poster, M: *The Mode of Information.,*(1990).
Prince Philip.: HRH The Duke of Edinburgh. *Men, Machines and Sacred Cows.,*(1982).

Radhakrishnan, S., Raju, P., T.: *The Concept of Man: A Study in Comparative Philosophy.,* (1960).
Radley, A.S.: *Mirror System Producing a Real Space 3-D Reflected Image of a Person (Hologram Mirror).* UK Patent granted - GB2454763.,(2009).
Radley, A.: Self as Computer - 2015.

Radley, A.: Humans versus Computers Systems and Machines; a Battle for Freedom, Equality and Democracy, keynote paper, Proceedings of the 6th International Conference in Human-Computer Interaction, Tourism and Cultural Heritage, (2015).

Rand, Ayn.: Atlas Shrugged., (1957).

Rand, Ayn.: The Fountainhead., (1943).

Reichardt, Jasia.: Robots: Fact, Fiction and Prediction., (1978).

Rheingold, Howard.: Tools for Thought. MIT Press, (1983).

Rheingold Howard.: Virtual Reality., (1991).

Roberts, Keith.: Machines and Men., (1973).

Rogers, Everett M.: Diffusion of Innovations. (2003).

Roheim , Geza,. Muensterberger, Warner.: Magic and Schizophrenia., (2006).

Rogaway, Pillip, The Moral Failure of Computer Scientists, The Atlantic, 2016

Rose, N.: Governing the Soul.

Rose, N.: Inventing Ourselves.

Ross, K.W., Kurose, James, F.: Computer Networking;   A Top Down Approach., (2012).

Roszak, Theodore.: The Making of a Counter Culture., (1969).

Routledge, Robert.: Discoveries and Inventions of the 19th Century., (1900).

Rucker, Rudy.: Mind Tools. Penguin Books, (1987).

Rucker, Rudolf., Povilaitis, David.: The Fourth Dimension: A Guided Tour of the Universe., (1985).

Rushkoff, Douglas.: Cyberia: Life in the Trenches of Hyperspace., (1994).

Russell, Bertrand.: Skeptical Essays. Unwin Hyman Ltd, (1963).

Russell, Bertrand.: The Problems of Philosophy., (1912).

Sagan Carl.: Dragons of Eden: Speculations on the Evolution of Human Intelligence., (1986).

Sagan, C.: The Demon Haunted World: Science as a Candle in the Dark., (1997).

Salinger. J.: The Catcher in the Rye., (1951).

Salomon, David., Bryant, D.: Handbook of Data Compression., (2009).

Sartre, Jean-Paul.: Imagination., (1962).

Sartre, Jean-Paul.: Being and Nothingness: An Essay on Phenomenological Ontology., (1943).

Shelley, Mary.: Frankenstein, or The Modern Prometheus. (1818).

Schopenhauer, A.: The World As Will and Representation., (1844).

Searle, John, R. : The Mystery of Consciousness., (1990).

Shannon, Claude, E.: A Mathematical Theory of Communication. (1949).

Shannon, Claude, E.: Theory of Secret Systems.

Singleton, W., T.: Man-Machine Systems., (1974).

Sutherland, I.: Sketchpad; A Man Machine Graphical Communication System. AFIPS Conference meeting, (1963).

Talbott, Steve.: The Future Does Not Compute: Transcending the Machines in our Midst. (1995).

Tanenbaum, Andrew, S., Wetherall, David. J.: Computer Networks (5th Edition)., (2010).

Thring, M.W.: Man, Machines and Tomorrow., (1973).

Toffler, Alvin.: Future Shock., (1984).

Tresch, John.: The Romantic Machine: Utopian Science and Technology After Napoleon., (2012).

Tuck, M.: The Real History of the GUI. Online article: http://www.sitepoint.com/real-histo ry-gui/. Retrieved (2013-08-13).

Notes on a link, comments on a relationship. - Ted Nelson

Everything that we formerly electrified we will cogitise. - Kevin Kelly

Tufte, Edward.: *Envisioning Information*.,(1990).

Tufte, Edward.: *The Visual Display of Quantitive Information*.,(2001).

Turkle, Sherry.: *The Second Self: Computers and the Human Spirit.*, (1984).

Turing, A.: *Computing Machinery and Intelligence*. Mind. (1950).

UK Patent Office Abridgements of Specifications: (1900-1901, 1904, 1925).

Universal Declaration of Human Rights. UN General Assembly. (1948).

Veltman Kim.: *The Alphabets of Life*, (2014).

Veltman Kim.: *Understanding New Media*, (2006).

Veltman, K.H.: *Linear Perspective and the Visual Dimensions of Science and Art*. Deutscher Kunstverlag,(1986). (http://vmmi.sumscorp.com)

Veltman, K.H.: *Bibliography of Perspective. (1975-1995)*. See online version : http://vmmi.sumscorp.com/develop/

Veltman, K.H.: *Sources of Perspective; Literature of Perspective (1985-1995)*; See online: http://sumscorp.com/perspective/

Verne, Jules.: *Twenty Thousand Leagues Under the Sea*.,(1870).

von Helmholtz, Hermann.: *A Treatise on Physiological Optics (Volumes 1-3)*., (1910).

Watson, Richard.: *Future Minds: How the Digital Age is Changing Our Minds, Why this Matters and What We Can Do About It.*, (2010).

Wells, Herbert, George.: *First and Last Things*.,(1908).

Wells, Herbert, George.: *The Shape of Things to Come*.,(1933).

Wells, Herbert, George.: *A Modern Utopia*.,(1905).

Wells, Herbert, George.: *World Brain*.,(1936).

Wertheimer, Max.: *Productive Thinking*. (1971)

Whitehead, Alfred, North.: *Process and Reality*.,(1929).

Wiener, Norman.: *God and Golem: Comments on Certain Points Where Cybernetics Impinges on Religion.*, (1990).

Wilhelm, Richard.: *The Secret of the Golden Flower: A Chinese Book of Life*.,(1945).

Wired Magazine: Complete Collection

Wittgenstien, L.: *Logisch-Philosophische*.,(1921).

Wittgenstein, Ludwig.: *Philosophical Grammar.*, (1969).

Wittgenstien, L.: *Tractatus Logico-Philosophicus*. ,(1922).

Wolfram, Stephen.: *A New Kind of Science*.,(2002).

Woolley, Benjamin.: *Virtual Worlds*., (1994).

Wurman, Saul.: *Information Anxiety*., (1989).

Wurster, Christian.: *Computers: An Illustrated History.*, (2002).

Yates, Francis.: *The Art of Memory*.,(2001).

Zamyatin, Yevgeny., Brown, Clarence.: *We.,(1921)*.

Zittrain, Jonathan.: *The Future of the Internet: And How to Stop It.*, (2009).

Truman: Then who am I? **Christof:** You're the star.

Truman: Was nothing real? **Christof:** You were real.

That's what made you so good to watch. [The Truman Show]

Appendix A) Private, Secret and Open-Thoughts

A secret-thought is a thought that occurs in the mind of an individual, and has not left the 'mind' of the thinker to enter another person's mind and/or machine's 'mind' (yet). Secret-thoughts may, in fact, be related to thoughts originating in other people's minds; but vital here is that nobody else yet knows, or can easily discover the contents of the same, or that the thought has been (or is being) thought by the thinker. Secret-thoughts are an individual's natural property alone. Others may be able to guess a secret-thought; but that is different from certain knowledge. With secret-thoughts the thinker is in (more or less) complete control over any communicated thought contents. A secret-thought is—bound in time—because what was once secret, may no longer be secret at some epoch in the future. Secret-thoughts are protected from discovery by others—and are hidden in some way. Secrecy is a state of being for the thought itself. Secret-thoughts, by definition, exist in a single mind—or no mind—in the case of 'lost' secret-thoughts.

Every open-thought was once a secret-thought; but has subsequently been communicated to other mind(s), or else written down and stored in a place freely accessible to others. Open-thoughts are essentially, social thoughts. Open-thoughts exist (potentially at least) in everyone's minds; and the originator may have little control over how, when, and to whom such thoughts are communicated. Both open and secret-thoughts may be singular or composite; and thus be comprised of thoughts and sub-thoughts copied from elsewhere, and link-to and/or subsume (or represent) many other thoughts/patterns.

What differentiates open from secret-thoughts is their state of discoverability—and in this respect a thought is only secret, if there can be no possibility of transfer to another mind (at a specific epoch). Writing down a thought in a public arena, would potentially nullify secrecy (in the future); and hence such an exposed thought may no longer be classified as secret, and because it is—potentially discoverable (it is a hidden/lost open-thought until then).

It is vital to recognise that not only original-thoughts start out as secret. When someone thinks/duplicates an unusual thought originated by someone else, then the fact that they are thinking this same thought, may constitute a secret—and hence a changed thought—by itself. What matters is whether another party is able to access unique/original thoughts (or has the possibility of so doing).

A third class of thought is identified as a private-thought; defined as a thought which has-been/will-be shared amongst a restricted group. Private-thoughts possess a special feature, in that they are distributed to a limited number of people; and hence some form of social sharing plus protection is implied; and in order to protect the status of a private-thought, and to prevent it from morphing into an open-thought. Discoverability is restricted and controlled by some mechanism/lock/key, plus social trust.

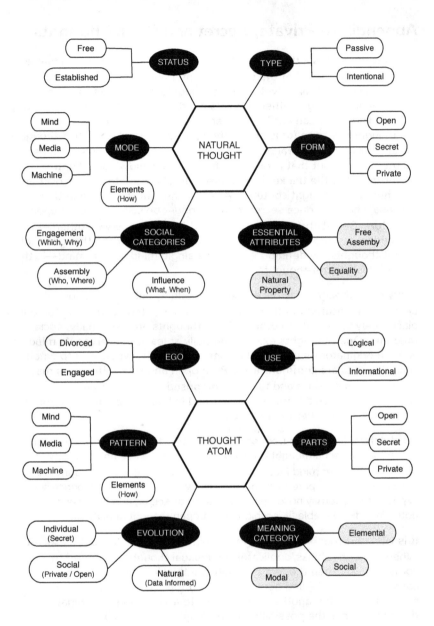

Somewhere we have bodies, very far away, in a crowded loft roofed with steel and glass.
Somewhere we have microseconds, maybe time left to pull out. ... jacked into a custom
cyberspace deck that projected his disembodied consciousness into the
consensual hallucination that was the Matrix.
Case fell into the prison of his own flesh. - W. Gibson

Appendix B) Total Secrecy / Privacy

It is insightful to ponder a little on the nature of secrecy and privacy...

To begin with, let us imagine that you are standing next to someone in a private location, before passing a real-world object to that person, and in a such manner that ensures (for argument's sake) that this same action cannot be overlooked / discovered. Accordingly, it is easy to understand - that this act is absolutely private. However things are not quite so simple - when you pass datagrams (messages, folders and files etc) across a remote wired / wireless communication system (aka the Internet). In particular, such a data-transfer may be visible and/or exposed to the actions of other programs/actors/people - and primarily because it has a public aspect - in terms of the visibility / accessibility of associated communications data. This is because the network itself is public - or open. For example, the packetised-data may be visible, and/or the wired/wifi communications may be observable/hackable; and/or the associated Internet traffic could be spied upon in some way etc.

Regardless of whether or not any exposed - or persisted - copies exist on the communication system itself (i.e. central copies) - one has to admit - that on an open-network - aspects of the live communication process may be visible to nth-parties. Hence communications must be (theoretically) no longer entirely private/secret - or at least in terms of the existence of any transferred packets etc; and most probably in terms of other aspects of the copy's form. Ergo, we are forced to conclude - that TOTAL PRIVACY / SECRECY - in relation to the - sum total of all aspects of a copies **form / content** - for such a digital communication process - is quite simply, IMPOSSIBLE TO ACHIEVE. Another problem, in our terms, relates to the mixing-up - of the media of storage, transfer and access - and in way(s) that likewise result in aspects of a copy's form being rendered publicly visible/accessible.

Our discussion implies that you (the owner of the copy) - plus the system designer(s) / operator(s) - must choose which aspects of the copy - and hence communication process as whole - to make secret/private. However certain aspects will, nevertheless, remain public! In other words - security is all about deciding which aspects of a datum-copy can be wholly removed from public view (aka beholder's share etc) - and which (inevitably public) aspects to protect using locking/blocking/concealment mechanism(s) etc. We can conclude that a secret / private communication process - taking place in a semi-public arena - always has public aspects - or facets - regardless of how powerful - or impenetrable - may be the protection mechanism(s).

The user's going to pick dancing pigs over security every time.
— Bruce Schneier

Appendix C) Secrecy Defined

What is **secrecy**, in-and-of-itself? And how do we keep something **secret?** What are the fundamental techniques for attaining/securing secrecy?

Unquestionably, these are fundamental questions (for any society) - and answering the same can help us to understand secrecy at a deep, and even philosophical, level. Ergo, we wish to come up with a strict definition for the term. In this respect, right away, we notice that it is necessary to protect an item by **concealing, blocking** and/or **locking** its specific material-form and/or inner-meaning from others. In other words we must prevent other people from **finding, contacting** and/or **knowing the item**. Obviously we can build a protective barrier (i.e walls) around the item (i.e place it in a safe/vault); and then create a locked door - being one that requires some form of password / secret-key in order to open. Alternatively, we can prevent any unwarranted person from reaching the item - by means of blocked/inaccessible pathways. Finally, we could hide the item in a secret location known only to ourselves - and the same being one that is - for some reason - difficult to see/find by other people.

But all of this begs the question - what is the common feature of secrecy - and can we identify any fundamental characteristic(s) - in terms of being able to attain it by means of a particular method? Put simply, attaining/defending secrecy - for any item - may be defined as protecting the material/virtual-form of a thing; or restricting its contents to the actual owner of the thing alone. In other words, we wish to protect the secrecy of the item - in terms of who can **see, know** and/or **change** it. The concept of secrecy is at the same time - and equally - **socially defensive** (broadest possible terms) and **socially restrictive** (narrowest possible terms). Above all, secrecy requires that the genuine entry-method(s) - or valid pathway(s) - used to reach the item's form/content - must be exceptionally well-defended (in social accessibility terms) - and remain so perpetually.

Ergo, any and all unauthorised pathways / surreptitious entry-methods must be untenable. Additionally - authorised entry-method(s) - must be of such a form / type / kind that they cannot be attained / guessed / stumbled-upon, or otherwise discovered/used by any unwarranted-party / breaching-technique (including statistical methods etc). In a nutshell, secrecy is the attenuation / whittling-down - or drastic reduction - of unwarranted accessibility options (entry-methods/pathways) for an item - whereby the (relatively scarce) authentic entry-method(s)/pathway(s) are perpetually out-of-reach to any and all unwarranted people/actors.

Amateurs hack systems, professionals hack people.
— Bruce Schneier

Appendix D)

Comparison with Traditional Cryptography

According to Fred Wrixen "The fierce competition that developed between cryptographers and their solution-seeking rivals became known as cryptography, from the Greek krypte - meaning 'secret or hidden', and either the word 'logos', meaning 'word', or 'ology' meaning 'science'. The term cryptography eventually encompassed the two competing skills: concealment by cryptography (krypte, kryptos, and graphia, 'writing') and revelation by cryptoanalysis, from krypte, or the Latin crypta, and the Greek 'ana' 'up throughout' and lysys, ' a loosening'. The roots of cryptography are various, and scholars believe that as languages develop among different societies, so do the tendencies to seek means of communications concealment."[ref. Codes and Cyphers]

It may be instructive to briefly examine some standard principles of cryptography - and in order to compare and contrast the ideas presented in the present book with those given by more traditional and/or standard treatment(s).

Overview of Encryption / Coding

We begin with a relatively straight-forward definition. According to Wikipedia: "**Encryption** is the process of encoding messages or information in such a way that only authorised parties can read it. Encryption does not of itself prevent interception, but denies the message content to the interceptor." So far so good - but I think we need to delve a little more deeply into the matter of what encryption actually is - how it is normally defined - and hence to examine it basic features / principles etc.

Firstly we have the plaintext - which refers to the message that will be put into secret form. The message may be hidden in 2 basic ways. Firstly, the methods of **steganography** conceal the very existence of the message - for example the first letter of each word in an apparently innocuous message spells out the real word (in our terms: metrical / symbolic representation - locking / concealment).

Using encryption on the Internet is the equivalent of arranging an armored car to deliver credit card information from someone living in a cardboard box to someone living on a park bench. — Gene Spafford

Steganography can be applied to electrical communications, such as a method that transmits a long radio message in a short spurt, and such methods are called **transmission security** (or in our terms: physical form representation locking / concealment and/or virtual form representation locking / concealment).

Secondly, the methods of **cryptography,** render the message unintelligible to outsiders by various **transformations** of the plaintext (in our terms: symbolic content representation locking / concealment).
Two basic transformations exist. In **transposition,** the letters of the plaintext are jumbled; their normal order is disarranged - and the meaning is obscured structurally. In **substitution,** the letters of the plaintext are replaced by other letters (for example) - and hence the meaning is obscured symbolically. Transposition and substitution may be combined.

Substitution systems are much more diverse than transposition systems - and they rely on the concept of a cipher-alphabet - which is a list of equivalents used to transform the plaintext into secret form. Single (mono-alphabetic) and multiple cipher alphabets may be used - two or more is named a poly-alphabetic substitution. Modern cipher machines can produce polyalphabetic ciphers that employ millions of cipher alphabets. Most ciphers employ a **key,** which specifies such things as the arrangement of letters within a cipher alphabet, or the means of shuffling on a transposition, or the settings on a cipher machine.

Among the systems of substitution, **code** is distinguished from **cipher.**

A code consists of thousands of words, phrases, letters and syllables with **codewords** or **codenumbers** (or more generally **codegroups**) that replace plain text elements (in our terms: descriptive content representation locking / concealment). In a sense, a code comprises a gigantic cipher alphabet. Whereby syllables and letters are supplied to spell out letters not present in the code. In ciphers, on the other hand, the basic unit is the letter or letter-pair (digraph or bigram) - sometimes referred to as **polygrams.** There is no sharp dividing line between codes and cyphers, and the latter shade into the former as they grow larger.

Stuxnet, a computer worm reportedly developed by the United States and Israel that destroyed Iranian nuclear centrifuges in attacks in 2009 and 2010, is often cited as the most dramatic use of a cyber weapon. - Barton Gellman

When it comes to privacy and accountability, people always demand the former for themselves and the latter for everyone else. - David Brin

APPENDIX   117

A useful distinction is that a code operates on linguistic entities; dividing its raw material into meaningful elements like words and syllables (descriptive content locking/concealment); whereas a cipher does not (symbolic / metrical content locking/concealment) - a cipher will split the letter **t** from the **h** in **the** - for example.

Likewise many of the sharp distinctions made in the present book are somewhat arbitrary. For example, consider the distinction made between **symbolic encryption** or metrical obfuscation using standard symbols that are transformed irrespective of encapsulated meaning(s) - verses coding - or descriptive, modal obfuscation using standard/non-standard symbol elements that map to non-standard ideas / structures / datum(s)). Ergo symbolic encryption deals with ostensibly 'meaningless' units - using standard symbols (which may be split into equally meaningless groupings - for example: transposed / substituted letter arrangements - before recombination once again etc). Wheres coding deals with linguistic elements (ie words) that have standard and/or masked / unusual / specially-introduced meanings.

 In a similar way to the standard description above - we pivot the distinction around **linguistic meaning(s)** - whereby coding is obfuscation of meaning at the conceptual level and/or introduction of unusual meanings. Put simply, ciphers obfuscate symbols, and coding obfuscates meaning. But there are no hard and set rules - because the two techniques are often used together / simultaneously and /or may sometimes overlap.

As an aside a standard term in cryptography is 'Symbol Cryptography'; defined as a form of cryptography in which plain-text is replaced by a symbol, such as a design or a written or printed mark. This differs from the definition of Symbolic Encryption as defined in this book - meaning generation of ciphers using letters and obfuscation of patterns of symbols using substitution and transposition etc - wherein no attempt is made to use standard and/or obscure / introduced meaning(s) to either conceal the message or content.

> We face cyber threats from state-sponsored hackers, hackers for hire, global cyber syndicates, and terrorists. They seek our state secrets, our trade secrets, our technology, and our ideas - things of incredible value to all of us. They seek to strike our critical infrastructure and to harm our economy. - James Comey

Privacy is not something that I'm merely entitled
to, it's an absolute prerequisite. - Marlon Brando

Appendix E) - Privacy Quotations

NSA BACKDOOR

Six years ago, two Microsoft cryptography researchers discovered some
weirdness in an obscure cryptography standard authored by the National
Security Agency. There was a bug in a government-standard random number
generator that could be used to encrypt data.

The researchers, Dan Shumow and Niels Ferguson, found that the
number generator appeared to have been built with a backdoor—it
came with a secret numeric key that could allow a third party to
decrypt code that it helped generate.

According to reports by the ProPublica, the Guardian, and the New York
Times, classified documents leaked by NSA whistleblower Edward Snowden
appear to confirm what everyone suspected: that the backdoor was
engineered by the NSA.

The result is that the trustworthiness of the systems we use to communicate
on the Internet is in doubt. The latest documents show that the NSA has vast
crypto-cracking resources, and a database of secretly held encryption keys
used to decrypt private communications.

Robert McMillan and David Kravets [wired.com]

PRIVACY RIGHTS

Given the apparent prevalence of this view (pro-spying) among the US
intelligence community, today's new Report and Recommendations of
the President's Review Group on Intelligence and Communications
Technologies—authored by a number of insider establishment figures—
comes as something of a surprise.

'There are sound, indeed, compelling reasons to treat the citizens of other
nations with dignity and respect,' the report says in an entire chapter
devoted to surveillance of non-US persons. 'Perhaps most important,
however, is the simple and fundamental issue of respect for personal privacy
and human dignity—wherever people may reside.'

Nate Anderson [arstechnica.com - 18.12.2014]

One of the original architects of the Internet wants to remind us that privacy
is a relatively new concept. 'Privacy is something which has emerged out of the
urban boom coming from the industrial revolution,' said Google's Chief
Internet Evangelist and a lead engineer on the Army's early 1970's Internet
prototype, ARPANET. As a result, 'privacy may actually be an anomaly," he told
a gathering of the Federal Trade Commission. [THE AUTHOR DISAGREES!]

"Those who surrender freedom for security will not have,
nor do they deserve, either one." — Benjamin Franklin

According to the New York Times, the NSA is searching the content of virtually every email that comes into or goes out of the United States without a warrant. To accomplish this astonishing invasion of Americans' privacy the NSA reportedly is making a copy of nearly every international email. It then searches that cloned data, keeping all of the emails containing certain keywords and deleting the rest, all in a matter of seconds. If you emailed a friend, family member or colleague overseas today (or if, from abroad, you emailed someone in the US), chances are that the NSA made a copy of that email and searched it for suspicious information.

The fantastic advances in the field of electronic communication constitute a great danger to the privacy of the individual. - Earl Warren

As a key part of a campaign to embed encryption software that it could crack into widely used computer products, the U.S. National Security Agency arranged a secret $10 million contract with RSA, one of the most influential firms in the computer security industry, Reuters has learned. Documents leaked by former NSA contractor Edward Snowden show that the NSA created and promulgated a flawed formula for generating random numbers to create a 'back door' in encryption products, the New York Times reported in September 2013. - San Francisco

An **advanced persistent threat** (APT) is a network attack in which an unauthorised person gains access to a network and stays there undetected for a long period of time. The intention of an APT attack is to steal data rather than to cause damage to the network or organisation. **The merger of cybercrime and advanced persistent threats**. In 2015 the Carbanak cyber-criminal gang stole up to $1 billion from financial institutions worldwide using targeted attack methods. - Kaspersky Labs (2015)

Journalism is not a crime.

Communication is not a crime.

We should not be monitored in our everyday activity!

The powers of Big Brother have increased enormously; and our expectation(s) of privacy have been reduced.

Democracy may die behind closed doors, but we as individuals are born behind those same closed doors, and we do not have to give up our privacy to have good government.

We don't have to give up our liberty to have security, and by working together we can have both open government and private lives.

Edward Snowden [Canada, 2014]

Once you've lost your privacy, you realize you've lost an extremely valuable thing. - Billy Graham

Appendix F) - TOR Network / Onion Routers

Tor is free software for enabling anonymous communication. The name is an acronym derived from the original software project name The Onion Router, however the correct spelling is "Tor", capitalising only the first letter. Tor directs Internet traffic through a free, worldwide, volunteer network consisting of more than seven thousand relays to conceal a user's location and usage from anyone conducting network surveillance or traffic analysis.

Using Tor makes it more difficult for Internet activity to be traced back to the user: this includes "visits to Web sites, online posts, instant messages, and other communication forms". Tor's use is intended to protect the personal privacy of users, as well as their freedom and ability to conduct confidential communication by keeping their Internet activities from being monitored.

Onion routing is a technique for anonymous communication over a computer network. In an **onion network**, messages are encapsulated in layers of encryption, analogous to layers of an onion. The encrypted data is transmitted through a series of network nodes called **onion routers**, each of which "peels" away a single layer, uncovering the data's next destination. When the final layer is decrypted, the message arrives at its destination. The sender remains anonymous because each intermediary knows only the location of the immediately preceding and following nodes.

- from Wikipedia - 28th January 2016

Personal Data Protection - Preventing Storage Loss

It is a fact of life that our personal computing systems, and also personal data are constantly under the threat of loss/destruction from all kinds of physical and virtual dangers (computer hard disc-drive failure, house fires, malicious viruses etc). The question of how to protect our most precious personal data should be high on our list of priorities. Many people backup their data onto network drives such as DropBox / iCloud etc. But dangers remain here also - and because these systems make no guarantees that you will be safe from data-loss; and in any case some viruses will not only erase your entire local hard disc drive and any attached drives; but also erase all data from all of your network drives as well. What to do?

It is difficult/impossible to suggest any completely fail-safe measures that you can take in order to protect your data, but I can make a few of suggestions related to the diverse measures that I undertake to protect my own data. In this respect, I always: A) backup my data to several hard-drives (stored at separate physical locations - including a couple of USB drives on my key ring that I always carry); and B) I make regular backups to network drives; and C) I regularly backup my data to optical DVD discs (stored at separate locations); and finally: D) for really precious personal data I still make certain that I have print-outs (i.e. pictures, documents, bank account details etc). Note that any/all of my digital backups may be susceptible to delayed or post-dated program startups for virus infections (that I do not know are present); hence any backup may be compromised - and I insure myself (partly) from this eventuality by making regular backups.

More and more, modern warfare will be about people sitting in
bunkers in front of computer screens, whether remotely piloted
aircraft or cyber weapons. - Philip Hammond

APPENDIX   121

Appendix G) - Internet Privacy

Internet privacy involves the right or mandate of personal privacy concerning the storing, repurposing, provision to third parties, and displaying of information pertaining to oneself via the Internet. Internet privacy is a subset of data privacy. Privacy concerns have been articulated from the beginnings of large scale computer sharing.

On the internet you almost always give away a lot of information about yourself: Unencrypted e-mails can be read by the administrators of the e-mail server, if the connection is not encrypted (no https), and also the internet service provider and other parties sniffing the traffic of that connection are able to know the contents. Furthermore, the same applies to any kind of traffic generated on the Internet (web-browsing, instant messaging, among others) In order not to give away too much personal information, e-mails can be encrypted and browsing of webpages as well as other online activities can be done traceless via anonymisers, or, in cases those are not trusted, by open source distributed anonymisers, so called mix nets. Renowned open-source mix nets are I2P - The Anonymous Network or TOR.

Control over one's personal information is the concept that "privacy is the claim of individuals, groups, or institutions to determine for themselves when, how, and to what extent information about them is communicated to others." Charles Fried said that "Privacy is not simply an absence of information about us in the minds of others; rather it is the control we have over information about ourselves." Control over personal information is one of the more popular theories of the meaning of privacy.

Some experts such as Steve Rambam, a private investigator specialising in Internet privacy cases, believe that privacy no longer exists; saying, "Privacy is dead – get over it". In fact, it has been suggested that the "appeal of online services is to broadcast personal information on purpose." On the other hand, in his essay The Value of Privacy, security expert Bruce Schneier says, "Privacy protects us from abuses by those in power, even if we're doing nothing wrong at the time of surveillance."

- from Wikipedia - 28th January 2016

The diverse threats we face are increasingly cyber-based. Much of America's most sensitive data is stored on computers. We are losing data, money, and ideas through cyber intrusions. This threatens innovation and, as citizens, we are also increasingly vulnerable to losing our personal information. - James Comey

We have built as a government something called the National Cyber Investigative Joint Task Force, NCIJTF, where 19 federal agencies sit together and divide up the work. See the threat, see the challenge, divide it up and share information. - James Comey

Protection of Access for the Copy Owner

In this book, we defined security as protection of access to an item; but largely for unsafe-actors. We did not deal with how to protect access to an item - for the actual owner - or protecting copies that are stationary or stored on the primary-network. Such protections fall under the remit of the network / system-owner; and obviously involve data backups etc.

The challenge in the digital economy is
that no chain is stronger than its
weakest link. - C. Weinberg-Tougaard

Appendix H) - Quotations

Information is power.

But like all power, there are those who want to keep it for themselves.

The world's entire scientific and cultural heritage, published over centuries in books and journals, is increasingly being digitized and locked up by a handful of private corporations. Want to read the papers featuring the most famous results of the sciences? You'll need to send enormous amounts to publishers like Reed Elsevier...

There are those struggling to change this. The Open Access Movement has fought valiantly to ensure that scientists do not sign their copyrights away but instead ensure their work is published on the Internet, under terms that allow anyone to access it. But even under the best scenarios, their work will only apply to things published in the future.

Everything up until now will have been lost.

That is too high a price to pay.

Forcing academics to pay money to read the work of their colleagues?

Scanning entire libraries but only allowing the folks at Google to read them? Providing scientific articles to those at elite universities in the First World, but not to children in the Global South?

 It's outrageous and unacceptable.

With enough of us, around the world, we'll not just send a strong message opposing the privatization of knowledge—we'll make it a thing of the past.

Will you join us?

Aaron Swartz (Guerrilla Open Access Manifesto) [2008]

In some ways, cryptography is like pharmaceuticals. Its integrity may be absolutely crucial. Bad penicillin looks the same as good penicillin. You can tell if you spread sheet is wrong, but how do you tell if your cryptography package is weak? The ciphertext produced by a weak encryption algorithm looks as good as ciphertext produced by a strong encryption algorithm. There's a lot of snake oil out there. A lot of quack cures. Unlike the patent medicine hucksters of old, these sofwtare implementors usually don't even know their stuff is snake oil. They may be good software engineers, but they usually haven't even read any of the academic literature in cryptography. But they think they can write good cryptographic software. And why not? After all, it seems intuitively easy to do so. And their software seems to work ok.

— Philip Zimmermann

The guardians of your company's cyber security should be
encouraged to network within the industry to swap information on
the latest hacker tricks and most effective defenses. - Nina Easton

APPENDIX   123

INTERNET FREEDOM

Despite the air of pessimism surrounding the Web Index 2013 launch in light of the
state spying controversies, Berners-Lee remained positive about the many good
things that are happening around the globe. According to the report, the Internet
remains vital in catalysing citizen action and real world change. Despite the fact that
30 percent of nations engage in targeted Web censorship and 'moderate to
extensive blocking or filtering of politically sensitive content', the Web and social
media played a big role in 'public mobilisation' in 80 percent of nations.

'This is not being spearheaded by political parties and NGOs', said Anne Jellema,
CEO of the World Wide Web Foundation. 'It's spontaneous and grassroots action
driven by social media.'

'I am optimistic', said Berners-Lee. 'I think the people will win. I have faith in people and
humanity as a whole. There's going to be some push back, but change will come in lots of
different ways—from activism, but also UN resolutions. Also from within government.
There are people that care about this stuff.'

PRIVACY RIGHTS

Given the apparent prevalence of this view (pro-spying) among the US intelligence
community, today's new Report and Recommendations of the President's Review
Group on Intelligence and Communications Technologies—authored by a number
of insider establishment figures—comes as something of a surprise.

'There are sound, indeed, compelling reasons to treat the citizens of other nations
with dignity and respect,' the report says in an entire chapter devoted to
surveillance of non-US persons. 'Perhaps most important, however, is the simple
and fundamental issue of respect for personal privacy and human dignity—
wherever people may reside.' - Nate Anderson [arstechnica.com - 18.12.2014]

NEW THREATS IN 2015

Precise attacks merged with mass surveillance. Animal Farm's targeted
cyber-attacks merged with DDoS attacks from the same threat actor, which is rare for
advanced targeted cyber-campaigns. - Kaspersky Labs (2015)

Threat actors add mobile attacks to their arsenal. Desert Falcons
targeted Android users. - Kaspersky Labs (2015)

New methods of data exfiltration. Satellite Turla was found to use satellite
communications to manage its command-and-control traffic. - Kaspersky Labs (2015)

The evolution of malware techniques. In 2015, GReAT discovered
previously unseen methods used by the Equation group, whose malware can modify
the firmware of hard drives, and by Duqu 2.0, whose infections make no changes to
the disk or system settings, leaving almost no traces in the system. These two
cyber-espionage campaigns surpassed anything known to date in terms of
complexity and the sophistication of techniques. - Kaspersky Labs (2015)

Appendix I) - Deception

Deception - or the action of deceiving or tricking another party into believing in the truth of one specific fact / thing - when the genuine fact / truth is altogether different - may be a kind of ultimate principle in security. Providing an illusion - of truth - by means of false appearance(s) is the art of a magician. But related methods may be the ideal way for anyone to hide / conceal aspects of what they are truly up to. We include here all kinds of misdirection - that is making the observer look elsewhere than where the real action/items is/are stored/exist(s). Accordingly, the use of decoys and/or false-targets are standard techniques. During the second world war, the allies used 'cardboard tanks/ships'; which were - quite literally - life-sized cut-outs of the real thing - that were designed to attract enemy fire away from the real target(s). This happens because the enemy waste bullets, bombs, fuel etc; and hence time and effort, chasing phantoms. Deception is likewise often used in the security field to misdirect the enemies attention away the real activities/data. In our terms, it is possible for either an attacker and/or defender to use deception.

An attacker can employ all kinds of deceptions to gain access to protected system gateways.

For example, the ATTACKER can:

A) Use: false/hidden LOGINS/IDs/IP/MAC values, DNS re-direction, or employ unusual/stealth network traffic identification techniques (VPN/packet spoofing) etc, and all to break into the system (attack or break-into physical / virtual gateways); or else:

B) Employ false-certificates / fake-keys / compromised-encryption to unlock cyphers (attack or break-into metrical gateways).

Likewise, for example, the DEFENDER can:

A) Use: false/hidden data traffic, honeypots, Deception Toolkits, counter-attacks, creation of noise / padded null values etc (closure of physical and virtual gateways); or else employ all kinds of false-meaning deceptions and coded truths to conceal / block access to the various kinds of system gateways.

B) Hide the true message in apparently innocuous content (i.e. rely on the beholder's share for protecting metrical gateways) etc.

> **Crypto-Joker**: It is important to realise that it is not just the defender who can employ cryptography in order to protect his/her own specific interests. For example an attacker can use a tool such as Crypto-Joker - which is a form of ransomware / malware - that installs itself on the target computer before encrypting everything on the hard drive and any connected network drives. Whereby the poor victim must then pay the implementer of Cryto-Joker before he/she can decrypt their own hard-drive and once more gain access to their own personal information.

Appendix J) - World-Wide Data Breaches

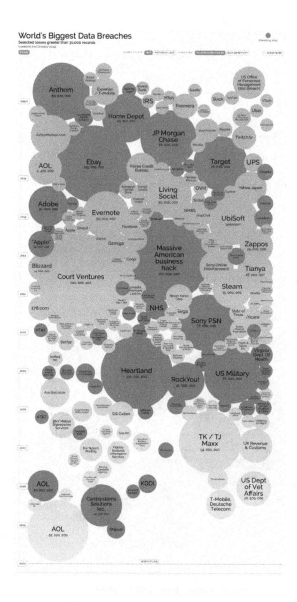

Major World-Wide Data-Breaches - 2004 - 2015 (rapid increase!)
Vertical Axis: Time. Bubble size: Number of Records Lost/Stolen.
Source: Informationisbeautiful.net

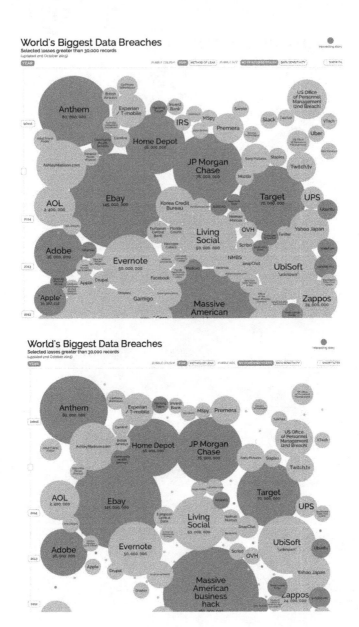

Data-Breaches from 2012 - 2015

Vertical Axis: Time. Bubble size: Number of Records Lost/Stolen.

Method of Leak: All kinds or accidents, errors etc (top); Deliberate Hacks (bottom)

Source: Informationisbeautiful.net

Appendix K) - Classic Hacks

A sampling of major system hacks - is as follows...

[1] **Multiple breaches occurred at the U.S. government's Office of Personnel Management** over nearly a year - and led to theft of data on 22 million federal employees that included the fingerprints of about 5 million. How they got in: using a contractor's stolen credentials to plant a malware backdoor in the network. Ergo, this is a classic example of a front-door plus back-door hack which could only have been prevented (one would suggest) by absolute security methods as follows:
A) address the specific reason(s) why/how the stolen credentials were attained - correct either physical(human) or virtual hacking method(s); and/or B) fully protect the front-door - by means of locking, blocking, and/or concealment mechanisms - combined with defence-in-depth etc.

[2] Two major health insurers, **Anthem** and **Premera**, were hacked, likely by the same actor, resulting in the largest theft of medical records to date. This must be some kind of back-door hack - and methods to shore-up central server data could (possibly) have prevented the same.

[3] Another major data-breach concerned **Ashley Madison**, the site for married people to find other married people with whom to have affairs. Its customer records were posted publicly, leading to much embarrassment, heartache and perhaps two suicides. Data compromised included 37 million customer records plus millions of account passwords - all made vulnerable by a bad MD5 hash implementation. Here it seems that the company had relied upon locking of a single metrical gateway - by means of weak algorithm(s) etc. Potentially a layered approach to metrical defences could have helped to prevent the same, and/or multi-factor authorisation, and/or the use of special diversity locks (something you have, something you know).

"He's not safe, but he's good (referring to Aslan, the Lion, in The Lion, the Witch and the Wardrobe)" — C.S. Lewis

Security is always excessive until it's not enough.
— Robbie Sinclair, Head of Security, Country Energy, NSW Australia

[4] Another data-breach occurred at **Anthem:** Whereby large amounts of data were compromised – including personal information about more than 80 million people. How they got in was by exploiting a watering hole attack that yielded a compromised administrator password. Once again a layered approach to security (defence-in-depth) may have prevented this kind of attack - although it seems that staff training / knowledge / discipline was largely responsible - and it is likely that such a human lapse requires a human response - in terms of more effective absolute security working practices.

[5] Yet another organisation hacked was **Premera.** Wherein data compromised included names, dates of birth, addresses, telephone numbers, email addresses, Social Security numbers, member identification numbers, medical claims information and financial information for 11 million customers. They got in by using phishing to lure employees to type-in domain sites that downloaded malware. Ergo, a number of questions must be asked - including: A) how did the attackers discover company employee details?; and B) Why were safe security protocols (i.e recommended secure working practices) not in place - or if they were in place - why were they not followed?

[6] Another hack happened at the **IRS**. Whereby data compromised included the Tax records for 330,000 taxpayers - which were subsequently used to collect bogus refunds. Attackers got in using apparently stolen credentials and knowledge-based authentication information they gained from the IRS filing and refund systems. This hack was discovered because attackers sent so many requests for old tax returns, that the IRS IT team thought it was a DDoS attack and investigated. Defence counter measures are as discussed above for stolen access authentication details.

[7] Another company that was hacked is **Slack.** Data compromised included a database of usernames, email addresses and hashed passwords and some phone numbers and Skype IDs etc.

> There are no secrets better kept than the secrets that everybody guesses. — George Bernard Shaw

> Security is an attempt to try to make the universe static so that we feel safe. - Anne Wilson Schaef

[8] A major hack also happened at **Experian** which was a data breach that affected T Mobile. Data compromised included the names, addresses, dates of birth and encrypted Social Security numbers and other ID numbers etc. The credit rating bureau, Experian, was hacked by exposing the personal data of at least 15 million T-mobile customers. Experian apparently held this pool of data unencrypted behind one common lock. A way to protect against this type of attack is to use defence-in-depth techniques and/or multiple aligned: locks, blocks, concealment mechanism(s); and/or multi-factor authentication.

[9] **Home Depot**: The company said 56 million payment cards details have been stolen, and later disclosed 53 million email addresses had also been pilfered.

[10] **JPMorgan**, the biggest U.S. bank said a data breach affected 76 million households and 7 million small businesses. It turns out the JPMorgan hack could have been prevented if it had consistently applied its own security standards. JPMorgan uses two-factor authentication to prevent this kind of attack (users need both their password and a one-time pin to get access), but one of the servers was never updated. Someone found the insecure server and used it to break into JPMorgan's network. Hence the JPMorgan hack didn't use a zero-day exploit.

This hack is particularly worrisome - happening at the the largest bank in the US and fifth largest in the entire world. Hackers breached 90+ servers achieving levels of penetration that affected 76 million households and 7 million small businesses. The corporation claims that no fraud has occurred, nor were customers' financial details compromised, just their names, emails, and phone numbers. Absolute Security methods could possibly have helped prevent this type of attack - specifically by providing multiple entrance gateways (and locking, blocking, concealment of the same) - requiring an attacker to pass through several such gateways before system access can be attained (defence-in-depth).

A **Safe** is a receptacle for the secure storage of items; and any safe has twin aspects; firstly an enclosed space completely covered by an enveloping barrier or unbroken set of armour-reinforced walls - and thus protecting any contained item(s); and secondly a **Lock** and **Key** - which is a method for fastening an entrance aperture into the enclosed space - whereby the lock is a sealed entrance aperture - or a mechanism for restricting access to only those persons who actually possess and may use the key to unlock the same aperture. In our terms - the (lock + key) represents a valid entry-method enabling an actor to traverse a system access gateway; and the (safe + lock) is part of the defence mechanism(s) employed by the communication system to prevent access to the same gateway by any unsafe-actors.

[11] Another data-breach happened at **Neiman Marcus.** Hackers accessed the debit and credit card information of customers who shopped at this chain between July 16, 2013 to October 30, 2013. Originally, the company estimated that as many as 1.1 million cardholders could have been affected. Once again, this looks like a back-door hack - using a compromised central-server (what else could possibly have had such a disastrous result).

[12] **White Lodging Hotel** hack. The hotel franchise management company that manages 168 hotels in 21 states suffered a data breach that exposed hundreds of guests' debit and credit card information in 2013. (central-server and/or point-of-sale (POS) system hack)

[13] **Michaels,** the nation's largest arts and crafts chain, reported a data breach at the end of January. The company said close to 2.6 million cards used in payments at their stores were potentially exposed between May 8, 2013 and January 27, 2014. (back-door plus central-server hack)

[14] In May, **Affinity Gaming,** which operates 11 casinos in Nevada, Colorado, Iowa and Missouri, announced they found evidence of a hack on the casino's debit and credit card system for non-gaming purchases. (central-server hack and/or point-of-sale (POS) system hack)

[15] According to a report from New York's Attorney General, 22.8 million private records of New Yorkers were exposed due to data breaches over the last eight years. The data breaches were reported by over 3,000 businesses, nonprofit organisations and government agencies. Intentional hacking exposed most of the accounts, accounting for 40% of the 5,000 incidents. Lost or stolen equipment, insider wrongdoing and inadvertent errors were also major factors. Hence physical gateways, or compromised access-devices and/or access-nodes were not sufficiently protected (multiple types).

[16] **P.F. Chang's China Bistro** reported a security breach that affected customers at 33 restaurants located in 16 states. The intruder may have stolen some data from certain credit and debit cards that were used during an eight-month period from October 19, 2013 to June 11, 2014.

"We live in a world that has walls and those walls need
to be guarded by men with guns." — Aaron Sorkin, A

The potentially stolen credit and debit card data included the card number and, in some cases, the cardholder's name and/or the card's expiration date. (central-server and/or point-of-sale (POS) system hack)

[17] **Community Health Systems** said information on 4.5 million patients data was stolen in a cyber attack that may have originated in China. The data breach may have impacted anyone who was a patient in a CHS hospital during the last five years. Hackers may have obtained the patient names, birth dates, addresses, telephone and social security numbers. (back-door and/or front-door combined with central-server hack)

[18] **Goodwill Industries** confirmed that a data breach in 330 of its stores may have compromised an estimated 868,000 debit and credit cards. Payment card information, such as names, payment card numbers and expiration dates, may have been compromised. (central-server / access-node / POS hacking)

[19] One of the biggest and most well-known hacks occurred at **Sony**. In early December, hackers leaked five unreleased movies online and some employees' Social Security numbers. The security firm Identity Finder found the hack exposed over 47,000 Social Security numbers, including over 15,000 current or former employees. In addition, these numbers appeared more than 1.1 million times on 601 publicly-posted files stolen by hackers. A significant number of files containing the Social Security numbers were accompanied by other personal information, such as full names, dates of birth and home addresses, increasing the chances of identity fraud. (back-door plus central-server hack)

[20] Another infamous hack occurred at **Apple**, whereby **iCloud Leaked Photos / Celebgate** etc. Out of all these hacking stories, this one stands as a clear reminder to the average person that even if they are doing nothing wrong, perhaps they do still have some things they wish to hide. This breach affected around 100 celebrities. Their private photos found the eyeballs of millions of Internet voyeurs.

"We all flee in hope of finding some ground of security"
— M.T. Anderson, The Kingdom on the Waves

"It is a fool of a shepherd who culls his dogs."
— Jefferson Smith, Strange Places

But the **iCloud** hack itself was not some great technological feat. It used publicly available information to identify its targets, and exploited known weaknesses in certain Apple products (in this case, Find My iPhone) that were ostensibly there to "help" law enforcement. Because 'Find My iPhone' doesn't limit unsuccessful login attempts, the attackers were able to make unlimited guesses on their targets' passwords. Hence a poorly protected virtual system gateway login is responsible. Because Apple decided weak encryption for iCloud accounts was a good idea, and also did not provide Two-Factor Authentication (2FA) protection for iCloud and iOS backups prior to this hack, anyone able to guess your password could see and use and share personal information. This particular attack could have been avoided in in a few different ways, notably by using multi-factor passwords, and/or by using some kind of packet sniffing and/or unusual IP address checking - and in order to lock / block / conceal system gateways from unsafe-actors.

[21] Somewhat surprisingly, **Snapchat** has been hacked. Snapchat provides an apparently secure (private) picture messaging service. This service has its users thinking the pics they send will self-destruct and disappear after they are viewed (even though they are stored on central server systems at least for a period of time between creation and looking/usage). However, in late 2013, Snapchat was warned about some exploits found by a white-hat cybersecurity research firm that could allow hackers to link usernames and phone numbers for use in stalking targets. The inevitable happened. Hackers posted 4.6 million users' personal information on a website, including real names, usernames, and phone numbers of both "private" and public Snapchat accounts. It is not difficult to imagine methods that would have prevented any pieces of user data from being linked, as well as the targeting of results from that. Extra layers of protection could be added to user data - and in order to lock/block/conceal appropriate system gateways. For example multi-factor authentication etc.

"Perhaps home is not a place but simply an irrevocable condition." — James Baldwin, Giovanni's Room

"Tradition becomes our security, and when the mind is secure it is in decay." — Jiddu Krishnamurti

[22] A hacker who broke into the AOL account of **CIA Director John Brennan** says he obtained access by posing as a Verizon worker to trick another employee into revealing the spy chief's personal information. Using information like the four digits of Brennan's bank card, which Verizon easily relinquished, the hacker and his associates were able to reset the password on Brennan's AOL account repeatedly as the spy chief fought to regain control of it. The hackers described how they were able to access sensitive government documents stored as attachments in Brennan's personal account because the spy chief had forwarded them from his work email.

[22] Intruders hacked into an email system used by the **Joint Chiefs of Staff** at the Pentagon, forcing the military to take if off line and "cleanse" it, according to a Defence Department official who spoke on condition of anonymity because they were not authorised to speak publicly. Indications are that the attack was conducted by another government, said the source. Experts are still analysing the scope of the attack and who was responsible for it. The intrusion forced the military to take down the network for unclassified information, although control of the system was not lost. The system is expected to be restored soon. Spear-phishing attacks trick people into opening infected emails that steal their network credentials and spread through a network.

[23] Russian hackers have broken into the **White House Email System**. As in many hacks, investigators believe the White House intrusion began with a phishing email that was launched using a State Department email account that the hackers had taken over, according to the U.S. officials. Director of National Intelligence James Clapper, in a speech at an FBI cyber-conference in January, warned government officials and private businesses to teach employees what "spear phishing" looks like." So many times, the Chinese and others get access to our systems just by pretending to be someone else and then asking for access, and someone gives it to them," Clapper said.

10 Golden rules of Information Security

[1] Have a focus on the information security program as a whole.
[2] Identify and manage risk.
[3] Follow the data.
[4] Apply defense-in-depth measures.
[5] Align with business products, services and objectives.
[6] Anticipate, be innovative and adapt.
[7] Establish a culture of security.
[8] Plan for a rainy day.
[9] Trust but verify.
[10] Tell the story and exert influence.

Monoculture - Monoculture is the case where a large number of users run the same software, and are vulnerable to the same attacks.

Practical Steps to Protect an Organisation from Data-Breaches

[1] Think broadly and deeply about security. Apply techniques such as defence-in-depth, and/or provide multiple access-controls that force an attacker to navigate several gateways before gaining entry to private areas/data.

[2] Use multi-factor authentication for system admins and users.

[3] Think outside of the box and beyond purely organisational boundaries. Look at exploits that relate to partner organisations and large-scale data bridges / data-feeds etc. Think about datum-copies - how many are there, who can see, know and /or change a copy, how long do they hang around. Consider also systematic pathways to copies - consider unusual and non-obvious pathways - including both at-rest and live copies.

[4] Employ methods to prevent Hackers performing system reconnaissance; especially in terms of how users / parties / systems interact with customers plus the centralised / remote systems - including centralised name resolution, POS gathering of information etc.

[5] Take steps to avoid Malware installation on system or customer computers. Think about locking/blocking/concealing related routes.

[6] Protect all kinds of system/data portals (i.e physical / virtual access-nodes/devices) - wherever they may be located.

[7] Protect all hardware / software aspects of Primary / Secondary Network(s). For example check for vulnerable domain controller(s) that could then be used to obtain access to POS systems etc.

[8] Protect all communication links / networks from being compromised. For example lock-down all non-essential NetBios sharing over all computer access-ports. Consider also environmental leakage etc.

[9] Block all communication methods not expressly used by legitimate system communications - ie. block FTP plus limit entity network access.

[10] Employ continuous Risk Management + Threat Modelling assessments / strategies / operations for all aspects of the organisation.

In the digital realm the concept of a copy - unlike a physical copy existing in the real-world - can be a perfect copy of the original (in form / content) - apart from the location at which the copy resides. Contrasted with everyday objects, the question of which copy is the real one arises; in addition to related questions like ownership protection and who has the publication rights etc. Ergo, in the digital world there may (in a sense) no longer be an original or true copy. These issues are often very difficult to resolve / determine - and may involve vast resources and sophisticated technical means, that are (for example) required to protect any private copy which exists in the public arena (ref moves, music etc).

Web of Trust - A web of trust is the trust that naturally evolves as a user starts to trust other's signatures, and the signatures that they trust.

[11] Avoid reliance on standard security "fallbacks" and/or stove-pipe mentality. For example, Payment Card Industry Standard - or PCI - compliance alone is not a risk management strategy. Only assets related to payment card processes are considered. Assets and implementation details that may pose the greatest risks to the organisation may fall outside of this scope and therefore not be adequately addressed if PCI alone drives business security decisions.

[12] "A security system is only as strong as its weakest link". Do not relay solely on bunker-style defences alone, consider also small-scale attacks such as decoys and human betrayal aka Snowden. If you install a large, strong gate at the front of your property, but a hole exists in the back fence large enough for a thief to enter, the gate can easily be bypassed.

[13] Many businesses that have experienced recent major breaches - employ encryption strategies. Unfortunately, encryption is often not properly implemented and deployed. Encryption in and of itself does not protect systems. A robust security strategy is required which protects entire systems in a comprehensive way in order for encryption to be effective. For example, an encryption algorithm and large key may become useless if you have the encryption key stored with the data. The hackers or malicious insiders will simply gain access to the system and use the key to unencrypt the data. Encryption is only one small (but important) piece in the larger jigsaw of comprehensive information security. Remember that unsafe employee working practices are often the most frequent (initial) entry method for any attacker.

[14] Consider why your central server data may be vulnerable, and what you can do to mitigate the risks surrounding any data-breach. Perhaps assume that a breach has already occurred, and consider if this compromises everything and why? Find ways to limit impact to a small number of records.

[15] Consider what information needs to be held centrally, and what does not need to be held in that way. As long as data is centrally stored, hackers will continue to reap massive windfalls. Perhaps the way we secure personal data needs to be flipped on its head. Instead of being centrally managed, the security of sensitive user account data could be (at least partially) decentralised/distributed.

Of all tyrannies, a tyranny exercised for the good of its victims may be the most oppressive. It may be better to live under robber barons than under omnipotent moral busybodies. The robber baron's cruelty may sometimes sleep, his cupidity may at some point be satiated; but those who torment us for our own good will torment us without end, for they do so with the approval of their consciences. — C. S. Lewis

Business Continuity Plan (BCP): A Business Continuity Plan is the plan for emergency response, backup operations, and post-disaster recovery steps that will ensure the availability of critical resources and facilitate the continuity of operations in an emergency situation.

Appendix L) - Architectonics of Cyber-Security Systems

In order to provide a comprehensive understanding of security; we first establish a set of axioms as follows:

< {1} **Security is protection of (social) access to an item.** >

< {2} Access (general) = Find, Contact and/or Know an Item >

< {3} Access (social) = See, Know and/or Change an Item >

< {4} Item = a real (physical) copy or a virtual datum-copy. >

< {5} Datum-Copy = a particular instantiation of a datum's pattern. >

< {6} Datum = A concept or idea of a thing, a pattern of meaning. >

< {7} Secret-Datum = social access is fully restricted - or **owner-restricted**. >

< {8} Private-Datum = social access is group restricted - by

single-copy-send (and potentially multiple instances thereof). >

< {9} Open-Datum = social access is for anyone - by **universal-send/receive**. >

< {10} Social Accessibility Status = a **secret / private / open datum**. >

< {11} Form = encapsulating media format - storage, transfer, access. >

< {12} Protect = Lock, Block and/or Conceal a copy from unsafe actors. >

< {13} Privacy Status = social accessibility status (for a datum-copy). >

< {14} Security Status = either **protected**; or **unprotected**: Privacy Status. >

< {15} A datum-copy's Accessibility or Privacy Status - may be either:

A) **Legitimate** (i.e posses secret, private or open status); or B) **Illegitimate**

(i.e fall into an undefined / hybrid category whereby privacy status is

unknown / compromised / changeable / unpredictable).>

< {16} Communication System = a system for transferring

datum(s) between persons and equipment. >

< {17} Communication = Transfer of discrete packages of meaning -

messages / datums - between people. >

Intrusion Detection: A security management system for computers and networks. An IDS gathers and analyses information from various areas within a computer or a network to identify possible security breaches, which include both intrusions (attacks

APPENDIX   137

< {18} Secret Communication = communication that preserves / supports a

secret-datum's secret accessibility status (i.e purely secret-datums). >

< {19} Private Communication = communication that preserves / supports

a private-datum's private accessibility status (i.e purely private-datums). >

< {20} Open Communication = communication that preserves / supports

an open-datum's open accessibility status (i.e purely open-datums). >

< {21} Socially Secure Communication = communication that protects

socially restricted access (secrecy or privacy) for the replicated meaning. >

< {22} Single-Copy-Send = communication of a datum with

guaranteed social security.>

< {23} Absolute Security TARGET (in the case of a private-datum) =

the single-copy-send of a private datum-copy from one

socially-restricted access-point to another on a provided

communication system (i.e. primary-network). >

*****

Evidently, we have 3 legitimate kinds of **Accessibility or Privacy Status** (secret, private, open) - associated with **3 types of Access Protection** (owner-restricted, single-copy-send, universal-send/receive).

Established is that, **security - or protection of social accessibility status** - is a time-bound property that must be provided by relevant security mechanism(s) - specifically:

• Carefully designed human or **manual working procedures** (i.e. particular social structures, regulated human-human interaction(s), prescribed data communication events/formats, specific social processes etc); and also by means of:

• Adequately secure **automatic and semi-automatic systems** - or the locking, blocking and concealment of primary, secondary, and tertiary network: system access gateway(s) / attack-surfaces.

Logic bombs - Logic bombs are programs or snippets of code that execute when a certain predefined event occurs. Logic bombs may also be set to go off on a certain date or when a specified set of circumstances occurs.

Overall, security - or access protection - equates to management of a datum-copy's form / content - existing on media of access, storage and transfer. Specifically, by one of the 3 methods identified: **owner-restriction**, **single-copy-send**, and **universal-send/receive**.

The primary aim of security is to prevent **legitimate** secret-datums from morphing into **illegitimate** private or open datums; and also to prevent legitimate private datums from morphing onto illegitimate open datums. Finally, legitimate open-datum access must be rendered generally accessible - whereby one seeks to protect accessibility for anyone / everyone (ref open-publication - see the companion book 'Self as Computer').

Now that we have developed a comprehensive definition of security, it is necessary to examine the environment(s) in which any particular datum-copy resides.

Typically present are **4 fundamental Categories of Computer Operation(s)** as follows:

• **PROCESSING** - deals with aspects of data: entry, gathering, movement, combination and transformation (local / remote);

• **STORAGE** - deals with aspects of data permanence (local / remote);

• **PRESENTATION** - deals with aspects of data connection, visibility and display (local / remote);

• **COMMUNICATION** - deals with aspects of data transfer (remote).

Now for each of the 4 types of computer operation; a legitimate copy may be either 1) secret; 2) private or 3) open. Ergo, there are (at least) **12 different kinds of protective techniques** (or sub-system(s)) that may be required for any particular information security system.

European Data Laws: The adoption of a new EU Data Protection Regulation (EUDPR) will set out to strengthen data protection legislation. It is likely to impose onerous new responsibilities on organisations, putting them at greater risk of falling foul of the law and subject to heavier penalties if they do. Renzo Marchini, special counsel at law firm Dechert LLP, says, "For example, in the UK there is currently no general obligation to report a data breach, while monetary penalties under the Act are limited to a maximum of £500,000, with a higher 'trigger level' for a large fine to be imposed". Andrew Miller, cybersecurity director at PwC, says that with data breaches becoming more sophisticated and their impact more damaging, boards need to review threats and vulnerabilities regularly.

Countermeasure: Reactive methods used to prevent an exploit from successfully occurring once a threat has been detected. Intrusion Prevention Systems (IPS) commonly employ countermeasures to prevent intruders form gaining further access to a computer network. Other counter measures are patches, access control lists and malware filters.

APPENDIX   139

For example: secret and private items on a communication system - often require 2 different kinds of protection (however both may use some of the same techniques). As stated, any related sub-system(s) are normally comprised of **automatic, semi-automatic** and **manual operating procedures** - and all of these must be managed appropriately (including interrelations / couplings etc) - and in order to provide effective protective security.

In the present book we have only explored one of the twelve sub-system protection types: specifically defence of **Private Datum-Copies existing on a Point-to-Point Communication System** (whilst superficially considering related aspects of data storage and presentation wherever necessary).

In conclusion, we can define **Absolute Security** (for a datum copy) as the **continuous protection** of social accessibility status with regards to:

A) Owner-restriction for secret-copies; or

B) Single-copy-send for private-copies; and

C) Universal-send/receive for open-copies.

Absolute security is an ideal (i.e measurable) protective status for any copy; according to the specific type of social accessibility that is to be maintained. Whereby absolute security has two components:

A) **Absolute Security Method(s)** - or continually working security: systems, rules, actors, networks, programs, defences and human / automatic operational procedures etc; that protect:

B) **An Absolute Security Target** - being of one of the 3 forms of social accessibility status (secret, private, open).

UK Surveillance: A new law setting out what powers the UK state will have to **monitor communications between citizens has been unveiled**. What new powers are being proposed? Communications firms - such as your broadband or mobile phone providers - will be compelled to hold a year's worth of your communications data. This new information will be details of services, websites and data sources you connect to when you go online and is called your "Internet Connection Record". There is no comparable legal duty to retain these records in the rest of Europe, the USA, Canada or Australia - this appears to be a world first. In simple terms, police say they want to be able to get at these records, going back a year, so that if they get a lead on a suspect, they can **establish more about their network or conspiracy**.

Appendix M) - Definition of Absolute in the Context of Security

You may sometimes here a security professional say something like: 'in the field of information security - (there are no absolutes) - except that (there are no absolutes)' - or words to that effect. Perhaps these same people do not realise that this statement is, in actual fact, an example of circular reasoning - or a logical statement that restates the premise as the conclusion. Anyway, a few eminent security experts - have expressed objection to the word 'absolute' in our book's title.

What I think these same experts are alluding to - is the impossibility of making any **absolute security predictions**; or attaining **perpetual - ever-lasting - security protection** in relation to information that is stored / transferred by means of networked computers. Such an interpretation is correct - because security is (and always has been throughout history) an arms race between those who seek to protect information and those who seek to circumvent those protections.

Today's best ciphers will doubtless be trivially broken in the future at some point. However, it seems that the dissent surrounding the word "absolute" is due to varied interpretations of what it means. In this essay I would like to fully define "absolute" in the context of security literature - and also the text of the present book in particular.

Let us begin by assuming that the term 'absolute security' - alludes to a system that is **permanently impregnable** for all time (i.e. it can never be broken into). That is **not** what I am claiming here for the meaning of the term absolute security - and for several reasons.

Earlier I had defined security as **protection of privacy status** for an item; and absolute security (for a private-copy) as single-copy-send - or no access whatsoever for unsafe-actors. Wherein **absolute security** is a kind of ruler or metric - one that indicates / reflects the specific **accessibility status** for the datum-copy.

An item is absolutely secure when it is - at the present epoch - out of reach of any unsafe actors - and there are no illegitimate copies. Henceforth, I would suggest that **absolute security is a measurable protective status** - and one that does not have to be possible - or permanent - in order for it to be a valid goal or metric in relation to a copy. Accordingly, we have neatly moved emphasis away from systems - and onto datum-copies - in accordance with the basic theme of the present book (security = protecting copies). However any copy-related insecurity must be the result of system failure(s) - so how/where do these problems arise?

Evidently, computing systems are extremely complex, varied and changeable - and many uncertainties can be the case for a datum-copy existing in a networked computing environment (even an ostensibly protected one). It follows that the privacy status for any item on a networked computer system - is a situation-specific property that may (quite possibly) change over time.

However this does not mean that we should adopt an attitude whereby we just shrug our shoulders whenever a leak/data-breach occurs. And then make the excuse that when it comes to security there are no absolutes - or even idealised metrics with which to judge security status. Systematic security is therein misrepresented as (forever) a contradiction in terms - something not even worthy of comprehensive definition and/or accurate measurement.

Inevitably, security experts encourage us all to install protective mechanisms, but often without providing the concordant means to adequately adjudge / measure if they are, in fact, working.

It would seem essential to first-of-all define the security goal for a private datum-copy - being **absolute security** (i.e. single-copy-send for a specific communication instance). A clear security target is required in order to have any chance of discovering whether we have attained it - or lost it - and why!

Surely we cannot be expected to just passively await the arrival of evil tidings in the form of system exploits - without full knowledge of what is the key goal / measure of communications security (single-copy-send). Unsurprisingly, such an 'no-absolutes' attitude pre-shadows a built in excuse for the designers of security systems. It gives them a get-out-clause; because they do not have to explain why or how the security targets failed - and because there are <u>none</u> - or at least highly specific ones like single-copy-send - complete with appropriate logical happenings.

We may conclude that successful exploits are not the result of a **lack of absolutes in security** - that is a wholly illogical argument - and because it renders uncertainty / lack-of-knowledge / poor defences as a valid excuse for failure. Whereby we put the symptom ahead of the cause. Rather we must accurately define **continuous security as the goal - which is itself a type of absolute** - or how else would you define successful protection of privacy - but as a kind of temporary permanence to be constantly achieved.

Please note, that I am not claiming here that we cannot have zero-day-exploits - or unknown-unknowns in terms of system design/operations - but rather that we should **wake up and smell the gunpowder.** We must seek to identify **bone fide** explanations for our security failure(s) - and not hide behind logical conundrums / meaningless mantras. Rather, we should embrace the truth - that it is a complete lack of precise, logical and measurable - **security targets** that holds us back.

Accordingly, we hereby define:

A) **The absolute security method(s) for a communications system** as consideration of every aspect of security to produce an all-round system that works coherently as a whole against all types of attacks, using the full gamut of known defensive techniques.

We do not mean that the system is permanently impregnable for all time (i.e. that it can never be broken). Absolute security is an attainable ideal (potentially), with a robust theoretical footing to back up its practicality and achievability.

We also provide a second related definition:

B) **The absolute security target for a private datum-copy** is defined as single-copy-send - whereby it is the communications system's absolute security method(s) that helps to deliver the same. Note that both definitions are ideal status metrics to be achieved and not permanent features that somehow self-perpetuate.

In conclusion, we need absolutes - and the concept of **absolute security** - not because it is a nieve dream-like state of system/data safety. We need the target(s) and method(s) of **absolute security** because these are idealised goal(s) - or assurance objective(s) - and reflect the very status values that we seek to measure our success and/or failure against. We could choose another grouping of words to represent the goal of **continuous security** (i.e comprehensive security). Nevertheless the underlying security metric is the same - a system that strives towards ideal and (hopefully) attainable security protection for our private information.

Appendix N) - Apple versus FBI

When U.S. Magistrate Sheri Pym ruled that Apple must help the FBI break into an iPhone belonging to one of the killers in the San Bernardino, Calif., shootings, the tech world shuddered. **Why?** The battle of encryption "backdoors" has been longstanding in Silicon Valley, where a company's success could be made or broken based on its ability to protect customer data. The issue came into the spotlight after Edward Snowden disclosed the extent to which technology and phone companies were letting the U.S. federal government spy on data being transmitted through their networks.

Since Edward Snowden's whistleblowing revelations, Facebook, Apple and Twitter have unilaterally said they are not going to create such backdoors anymore. **So here's the "backdoor" the FBI wants**: Right now, iPhone users have the option to set a security feature that only allows a certain number of tries to guess the correct passcode to unlock the phone before all the data on the iPhone is deleted. It's a security measure Apple put in place to keep important data out of the wrong hands. Federal prosecutors looking for more information behind the San Bernardino shootings don't know the phone's passcode. If they guess incorrectly too many times, the data they hope to find will be deleted. That's why the FBI wants Apple to disable the security feature.

Once the security is crippled, agents would be able to guess as many combinations as possible. Kurt Opsahl, general counsel for the Electronic Frontier Foundation, a San Francisco-based digital rights non-profit, explained that this "backdoor" means Apple will have to to write brand new code that will compromise key features of the phone's security. Apple has five business days to respond to the request.

What does Apple have to say about this? Apple CEO Tim Cook said late Tuesday that the company would oppose the ruling. In a message to customers published on Apple's website, he said: "We can find no precedent for an American company being forced to expose its customers to a greater risk of attack. For years, cryptologists and national security experts have been warning against weakening encryption. Doing so would hurt only the well-meaning and law-abiding citizens who rely on companies like Apple to protect their data."

Back in December, Cook defended the company's use of encryption on its mobile devices, saying users should not have to trade privacy for national security, in a broad interview with 60 Minutes. In the interview, Cook stood by the company's stance of refusing to offer encrypted texts and messages from users. **What does this mean for the next time the government wants access?** The order doesn't create a precedent in the sense that other courts will be compelled to follow it, but it will give the government more ammunition.

What do digital rights experts have to say? There are two things that make this order very dangerous, Opsahl said. The first is the question it raises about who can make this type of demand. If the U.S. government can force Apple to do this, why can't the Chinese or Russian governments? The second is that while the government is requesting a program to allow it to break into this one, specific iPhone, once the program is created it will essentially be a master key. It would be possible for the government to take this key, modify it and use it on other phones. That risks a lot, that the government will have this power and it will not be misused, he said.

And the lawmakers? Well, they are torn. Key House Democrat, Rep. Adam Schiff, D-Calif., says Congress shouldn't force tech companies to have encryption backdoors. Congress is struggling with how to handle the complex issue. On the other side of things, Senate Intelligence Committee Chairman Richard Burr, R-N.C., and Vice Chair Dianne Feinstein, D-Calif., say they want to require tech companies to provide a backdoor into encrypted communication when law enforcement officials obtain a court order to investigate a specific person.

What now? This could push the tech companies to give users access to unbreakable encryption. To some extent, it's already happening. Companies like Apple and Google — responding to consumer demands for privacy — have developed smart phones and other devices with encryption that is so strong that even the companies can't break it.

- Natilie DiBlasio and Elizabeth Weise - USA Today (February 17th 2016)

Apple Co-founder: 'I'm on the Privacy Side' of Apple vs. FBI

Apple co-founder Steve Wozniak appeared on CNBC's *Power Lunch* today to discuss the company's ongoing battle with the Federal Bureau of Investigation over whether Apple can, and should, build a new version of its operating system to allow the government agency access to data stored on a user's phone. "I'm definitely against that. I don't think that the phone should have backdoors," said Wozniak, using the industry term for an often-secret means of authentication for otherwise secure software. "I believe that Apple's brand recognition and value and profits is largely based on an item called trust. Trust means you believe somebody. You believe you're buying a phone with encryption. It shouldn't have hidden backdoors and ways that you don't know what's going to happen in the future."

What if you're a terrorist, though? CNBC's on-air journalists pressed Wozniak. "I don't believe that protects terrorist. There are other methods of doing investigation. We're talking about one case or a general category of cases, which is, you know, basically everybody—there's a backdoor for everyone and if that gets abused it could be conquered by hackers. It could be future people that run companies like Apple [who] decide to use it in ways they shouldn't." Wozniak went on. "Privacy has a good bearing. I grew up and was kind of taught that the Bill of Rights was really absolute core values that we should have. And now I find out, oh, well, we can just sort of disagree and go around them anytime we feel like it." Precedent plays a part when it comes to violating someone's privacy, Wozniak said, acknowledging that he has chosen to live his life in the public eye. "I think with court orders and whatnot that Apple would respond in an individual case. However the case is more like: Should you build in a backdoor that you can always find out what somebody had…they cannot have a realm of privacy, and I'm on the privacy side." He added: "In a sense, technology has won a lot of the battles [between] human versus technology. We should hold out what we can for the human." - Fortune (18th February 2016)

Skeleton-Key: In the real-world, a skeleton key is a key that has been filed or cut to create a master that can be used to unlock a variety of different locks. Similar techniques are possible in the cyber world. For example, several major governments continue to force system manufacturers and software companies to build in wide-ranging back-door access (for themselves) to systems everywhere - claiming that these 'Skeleton-Keys' will help them to keep citizens safe. But opponents call this an unacceptable invasion of privacy - and the beginning of the slippery-slope to George Orwell's world of '1984'. However the security gains - provided by any backdoor - may be an illusion, because the same skeleton key will - in all-likelihood - be used by Hackers as well. Many security experts say that there is no such animal - as a completely secure system - which at the same time has backdoor access provided by a skeleton key.

Appendix O) - Processing Atomicity / Complexity

Networked computers (in general) have advanced to the stage where they are - quite literally - beyond the (complete) understanding of any single human, or even a large organisation of humans. Our degree of **personal familiarity with** and/or localised knowledge of - all of the **vast multitude(s) of low-level implementation details** (and their combined effects for a particular data-processing path) may be very small / non-existent. And so we must **take it on faith** - that the top-level 'marketing' promises of what these (potentially) boundless processing units do - is (always) identical to what is claimed for them. But it may often be the case - that even the designers cannot foresee how the individual processing units will work in reality - and/or what will be the precise outcomes of there operation in any specific use-case scenario.

We have processor 'chips' containing billions of components, working on computers containing hundreds of millions of lines of code - code that exists inside many different kinds of programs (that may or may not be running on the same device simultaneously - and often sharing memory and system resources etc). Plus we often have remote-actors (humans, programs) using networked machines and influencing local events and processes etc; and everything connected to hundreds of millions of other networked computers etc. These complexities and fragmentary logic paths - **render into a fiction the atomicity of personal computers, device(s), programming operation(s) etc**. What to do?

Perhaps only to - combat lack-of-knowledge / uncertainty - with constant data-gathering, knowledge acquisition etc; and by employing specific monitoring system(s) - both automatic and human types. Plus by reading related news stories, and by staying up-to-date on the latest security exploits / defence-techniques / reports / surveys etc. Good luck!

Appendix P) - Privacy and Security Relations
(opposite page)

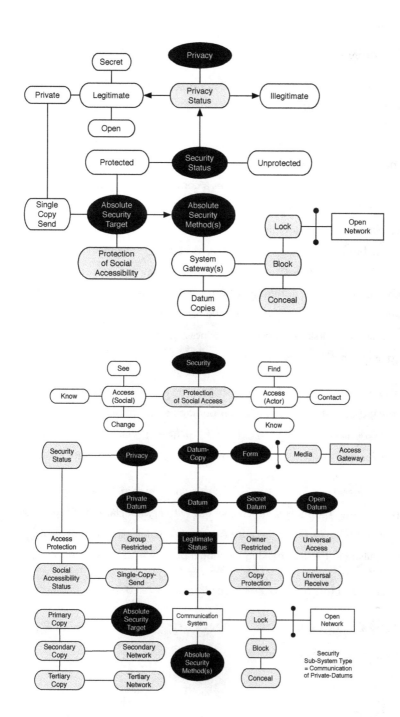

Review of Alan Radley's book 'Absolute Security'

For many years I have finished my presentations on cyber and risk with a slide entitled:

"And in this business there are NO ABSOLUTES" and I meant just that........like me Alan Radley espouses that no single or group of design/defensive measures deliver a complete cyber defence....rather the **whole system must be secure** by design, implementation and operation. Alan examines the concept of absolute security in depth with some fascinating insights into what he considers could and should be an individual's technological human right to privacy and secure communication. Ultimately he steers clear of just how he proposes to achieve what he claims is eminently achievable....absolute security remains tantalisingly obscure.....for now perhaps. The question 'secure against what'? remains unanswered.

Nevertheless despite some pretty utopian ideas, this book contains much that is thought provoking if perhaps some of his more philosophical concepts are unlikely to gain traction in our world driven by commercial considerations and the power of national security agencies.

The Appendices to this book are particularly rewarding reading, particularly Appendix E which lays out with crystal clarity the extent to which the US National Security Agency is involved in technological surveillance, thereby making individual privacy a 'lost' concept.

I commend this book to a wide readership. Well done Sir, more please.

Tony Collings OBE

Chairman The ECA Group

Absolute Security: Theory and Principles of Socially Secure
Communication; this book is a very concise body of work, that belies
its length for the practical application of useful data in a highly
complex area. Beyond its obvious sage advice with working diagrams
and imparted wisdom I particularly like the implied moral assertion
that the state undermining best IT security practice is to the detriment
of all. Further this should be required reading for anyone providing
third party services whereby their security claims cannot be held up
without transparency. Ignore this work at your peril.

Christian Rogan

Vice President, Business Development,
Royal Holloway Enterprise Centre,
Royal Holloway University of London, Egham, Surrey, UK.

This is a unique piece of work which correctly recognises the
socio-economic implications of modern day embracement, and
dependency on technology, and the ever present interface between
man-and-machine. The book provides the reader with an accurate
and objective view of the life-cycle of the exposures and
vulnerabilities which are associated with the technological shadow
cast over all individuals, and organisations. As an Expert Witness in
the discipline of Digital, this publication also provides very useful
descriptions in 'people-speak' and includes very accurate definitions
of the complex, transposed into understandable terminology.
This is an excellent read, and deserves a place on every security
professional's bookshelf who is seeking a balanced and objective
view of the current, and futuristic Cyber Security Landscape.

Professor John Walker
HEXFORENSICS – Digital Expert Witness
Visiting Professor at Nottingham Trent University

In Absolute Security: Theory and Principles of Socially Secure Communications, Dr. Radley exhibited an extraordinary passion for cybersecurity and privacy in the mold of the principles that conform to secure and just society.

In a world full of privacy breaches, Radley timely develops a framework that delves into complexity of technical and human-centric factors that affect our perception of privacy and cybersecurity. I recommend this book to everyone who is interested in making our cyber world more secure.

Vitali Kremez - **CISSP (A), CEH, CFE, CNDA, C-CPA**

Cybercrime Investigative Analyst,
New York County District Attorney's Office.

It is not very often that one is exposed to a work that is truly ground breaking in a field, but "Absolute Security" is one of those works. Rather than expounding on the implementation of security as many do, Dr. Alan Radley astutely asks (and then suggests an answer for) the rather naive, yet deceptively complex question "What is security?", or more precisely "How does one characterize a communication system that provides secure (private) data transfer?" As Dr. Radley examines this question, the reader becomes aware that the answer is much more elusive than one first assumes. As Dr. Radley builds a working compendium of definitions needed to examine the issue, the reader becomes more and more aware that the current vernacular is insufficient for discussing secure communication at a philosophical level, and if we cannot agree on what it means to be secure or private in thought, how can we accomplish it in act? It is here, laying the foundation of formal definition of socially secure communication, that Dr. Radley's work "Absolute Security" is groundbreaking and will no doubt be referenced by many works to come.

Michael Lester, **MSEE, MBA, CIPP/US, CISM**

Chief Information Security Officer / Vice President,
Magenic, Greater Minneapolis-St. Paul, USA.

According to Skinner (1953) human behaviors are linked with learning responses or conditioning, thus, leadership is a similar concept; even so, the result can have far reaching consequences. This perspective has into itself elements of a major strategic strategy and demands a substantial understanding of power use, and current technologies. The purpose of culture is to play as a stabilizing counter to any new change or rapid adjustment to the culture's values (Schein, 2004). The demand to provide coherent communication begins with leadership, management, and team members, which involves an advance understanding of team dynamics. The five layers of dysfunction within a team environment are (a) absence of trust, (b) fear of conflict, (c) lack of commitment, (d) avoidance of accountability, and (e) inattention to results (Lencioni, 2005).

The need to educate future leadership on various topics related to security, technology and compliance mandates the need to provide concrete and directive guidance in strategic adoptions of new technology, which enables growth (Watchorn, 2014). Tapscott (2011) states, that as each generation understands the digital lessons from the previous generations, the ability to overcome outdated security, social, and economic policy changes become enhanced by each generation's mistakes or assumptions. The book "Absolute Security" provides a clear-contextual approach to think about security related discussions from a multi-organizational approach, which often demands advance leadership skills. The strength of any security model depends on how each layer of security supports the inheritable aspect of the security conservation principle (Watchorn, 2014). I highly recommend this book for individuals interesting in understanding the challenges facing the security and information assurance specialist. Dr. Radley's direct approach provides an excellent read and can enable valuable insights into an extremely complex topic such as security.

Dr Merrick S. Watchorn - DMIST

Chief Cyber Security Analysis (Cloud SME),

Science Applications International Corporation (SAIC), Virginia, USA.

Reference(s):

Lencioni, P. (2005). Overcoming the five dysfunctions of a team. San Francisco, CA: Jossey-Bass Printing, Inc.
Schein, E. H. (2004). Organizational culture and leadership. (3rd ed.). New York, NY: Jossey-Bass Printing, Inc.
Skinner, B. F. (1953). Science and human behavior. New York, NY: The Free Press.
Tapscott, D. (2009). Grown up digital. New York, NY: McGraw-Hill Publishing, Inc.
Watchorn, M. S. (2014). Cloud adoption: A qualitative explorative multi-case study of the decision-making process by it leadership. University of Phoenix, School of Advance Studies.

For someone with over 20 years in IT Security and almost 40 years in ICT it is invigorating to read a book that introduces terminologies that would resonate with the academic world and is not burdened with technical jargon.

Reading Absolute Security also raises optimism that as an industry we have a chance in the imbalanced battle against cyber criminals. This also means that the statement 'there is no such thing as 100% secure' might be proven wrong.

An excellent read and would definitely recommend this to our AISA members as a read to get a different perspective on security.

Arno Brok

Chief Executive Officer

Australian Information Security Association (AISA)

Absolute Security is a brilliant book! Did it make me wiser? I say it did, however, it depends on the angle you are reading it from, your expectations and probably your background. You cannot suspect what is coming when you start reading. Definitely a very interesting approach on Information Security. One thing is for certain, this piece of work is not for the light-hearted.

Pantazis Kourtis

Member of the Board of Directors

London Chapter at ISACA

www.ingramcontent.com/pod-product-compliance
Lightning Source LLC
Chambersburg PA
CBHW071248050326
40690CB00011B/2308